P9-DCJ-939

BUT YOU SEEMED SO HAPPY

Also by Kimberly Harrington

Amateur Hour

BUT YOU SEEMED SO HAPPY

A Marriage, in Pieces and Bits

—

KIMBERLY HARRINGTON

HARPER

An Imprint of HarperCollins*Publishers*

BUT YOU SEEMED SO HAPPY. Copyright © 2021 by Kimberly Harrington. All rights reserved. Printed in the United States of America. No part of this book may be used or reproduced in any manner whatsoever without written permission except in the case of brief quotations embodied in critical articles and reviews. For information, address HarperCollins Publishers, 195 Broadway, New York, NY 10007.

HarperCollins books may be purchased for educational, business, or sales promotional use. For information, please email the Special Markets Department at SPsales@harpercollins.com.

FIRST EDITION

Library of Congress Cataloging-in-Publication Data has been applied for.

ISBN 978-0-06-299331-1 (pbk.)
ISBN 978-0-06-314300-5 (Library ed.)

21 22 23 24 25   LSC   10 9 8 7 6 5 4 3 2 1

This book is dedicated to everyone struggling in a good enough relationship with a good person (that person can be you).

How to Give Unsolicited Advice to a Friend Who's Just Announced Her Divorce

Don't.

Contents

ME

MARRIAGE

"DIVORCE"

Preface: My Little Homewrecker

When you tell people you're writing a book it's not unusual for them to ask what that book is about. I've found that their reactions to my answer provide a peek into what I can expect out in the larger world. Because people can't control what their faces do, no matter how hard they try. They think they're modulating their tone of voice, but they are surprisingly . . . not. And depending on the topic, the reactions are so automatic and visceral that they're just suddenly there, subconscious verbal burps.

When I was writing my first book focused on motherhood, I would say as much: "I'm writing a book of essays and humor pieces focused on motherhood." Boom. Straightforward. The reactions told me everything I needed to know. Most women who were mothers drew closer and asked questions. Most men, regardless of their parenting status, usually responded with a very uninterested-sounding "Oh!" or nodded in a way that said, "I will never read your dumb boring girl book."

Those reactions neatly summed up what was at play in the world, that women writing about women's experiences would only be interesting to women. And motherhood specifically? Forget it. Only in America could something experienced by eighty-five million people be considered niche.

But those reactions couldn't have prepared me for the

reactions to this book. Because when you're writing about mother-hood, it is safe to assume motherhood is an experience some women want to have on purpose. And it's an experience, at least on a superficial Hallmark-card level, that our culture approves of. Or to put it another way, a book about motherhood is harm-less. It's a book that will affect the world not at all. But when you tell people, as I haltingly did, that this book would be about "Marriage . . ." then mumble ". . . and divorce, uh, my divorce"?

Well.

Divorce is something no one goes looking for or grows up dreaming of experiencing one day. Our culture disapproves of divorce. It judges divorce and everyone involved. Divorce is an opportunity for people to wonder if you couldn't have done a bet-ter job not just with your marriage but with your entire life. So. This book, and by extension me and my divorce (which, spoiler alert, still hasn't happened as of the completion of this book), might prove to be dangerous and possibly contagious. This book sounded like a homewrecker.

People took the topic of my book personally. Which is fit-ting since people take other people's divorces personally. Even though I wanted to blow up how people talked about divorce, examine how I felt about my marriage ending, and even make fun of both marriage and divorce in general, I was the one who was still mumbling the word *divorce* in polite conversation. As if it was (mumbles) *cancer* or (mumbles again) *prison.*

Some of that hesitation came from knowing I would have to manage what came next. And what came next was always some version of this: :(

There might be an "Oh *wow*" said in a way that meant "Oh wow oh shit I wished I hadn't asked that question." Or the in-evitable, "Aw, I'm sorry," which made me want to punch a wall.

Because then I'd respond with, "Well I'm not!" which sounded like I was trying too hard or like my future ex-husband was a terrible person or our marriage had been a disaster, and none of those things were true. And then there we'd be, two tight smiles in a face-off, pretending like we weren't marinating in mutual bad feelings.

What a perfect way to convince someone to buy your book.

The implication behind all of this was, "*Why* write about *that*?" And also: "Ick."

Why, indeed. Why put my family through this when we were, in fact, still going through it? Why examine something so uncomfortable and bad? *Was* it always bad? Why do this to my kids when I already said I never wanted to go through the mental gymnastics I had put myself through on my first book, when I wondered why I focused so much on protecting them day-to-day but then would turn right around and write about our lives for complete strangers? Why dredge up the past? (People really hate all the dredging up of the past! Stuff that shit down where all the feelings go!)

The answers are likely not all that surprising if you've been through or are going through anything like this currently. I was desperately trying to find meaning in a relationship that had spanned half my life. I was trying to understand what it meant to enter into an arrangement as serious and theoretically permanent as marriage when I was still in my twenties. I wanted to know why I thought that was a good idea and why everyone around us thought that was a good idea, too. I wanted to understand what this all meant for me now, a woman who was about to be single and entering her fifties in America of all places, a country that largely perceives older women as clueless, sexless, useless, and shrill. I wanted to either stop being angry at myself or find new things to get even angrier about. I wanted to move the needle on my thoughts and emotions past the I Hate Everything red zone I'd been stuck in for two years. I wanted to explore whether or not I really knew "everything" and was very clear on "what went down" in my marriage, as I had convinced myself over time. More than anything, I wanted to make the case this had all meant something, anything. I wanted to understand who I was, who I am, and who I might be going forward.

It became clear to me early on that others were also trying to find meaning in their relationship struggles. They were trying to figure out if "happy enough" was good enough. More than anything, they just wanted to talk about it, but nobody would talk about it with them—at least not openly or honestly or without platitudes or judgment. We all hear the dramatic stories of divorce, but we don't hear much about boring divorces. Or perfectly okay divorces. Or divorces that simply signify a relationship has run its course and is now complete. Because if there aren't affairs, custody battles, nervous breakdowns, and an overall sense of humiliation then who cares?

As I discovered, a lot of people do.

The idea behind this book took shape just weeks after we announced our divorce straightforwardly and to as many people as possible. In that announcement we also shared we would continue living together for the foreseeable future. Our children were teenagers and our time with them was fleeting. Or so we thought. Our announcement took place in a pre-pandemic world, where school happened in person, children moved out at eighteen, and transitions were inevitable. With parenting they say the days are long but the years are short. But now the days are years and time is meaningless.

What became crystal clear to me in the wake of our announcement was that the simple act of being honest and open about our situation, choosing not to follow the expected script for how marriages typically dissolve, and refusing to act ashamed about any of it had kicked off a larger conversation. Friends who had felt ambivalent discussing their marriages texted me, asking if we could talk. Friends who were *already separated and hadn't told anyone* reached out. More than one work call got derailed as someone spilled their guts to me about their marriage or their fears over their career imploding because they were getting older and suddenly this was all intertwined. Most of the people I knew had married later, had kids later, and now it was all intersecting—suddenly they were middle-aged, with kids still at home, realizing their marriages were either going to implode or just slowly bore them to death.

I am not a champion for divorce. I spent the majority of my life running from it, both as a teenager and an adult. I am not a divorce evangelist. I don't think divorce is a wonderful idea and everyone should run right out and get one. I mean, *I* haven't even gotten one yet. If I'm an evangelist for anything, it's for all of us to think a bit more deeply about marriage and why we care so much about it. And if we find ourselves facing the end of a marriage, maybe we'd bend just a little less to the social pressures around us and do what's best for ourselves and our families.

A marriage doesn't just happen suddenly. We ramp up to marriage. We meet, we date. We get engaged, we have a wedding, then the marriage begins. Some would argue that a marriage only truly begins after a certain number of years or the birth of a child. But when a marriage is over, we don't ramp back down. We expect a marriage to end, a divorce to be final, and the relationship to be pushed off a cliff.

Although Jon and I didn't set out with the intention to evolve our marriage at the same time we were ending it, that's what happened. Along the way I wondered: Was it possible to truly still be a family while no longer being a couple? Did I think someone was going to tell us "no" (sometimes it felt like it)? Could we want the best for each other even when that "best" wasn't each other? Could I examine my own role in the unraveling of our marriage without defensiveness or anger (ha ha, probably not!)?

It was about more than having an amicable divorce, a toothless way of saying "we mostly don't want to knife each other." And it was about more than friendship, it was about kinship. A kinship that represented parenting and partnership, family and friendship, free of the weight of an interdependent, romantic bond.

I'm making it sound like we approached this phase with purpose, sitting cross-legged together at therapy, mooning over our "process" and scribbling in a common journal. That is . . . absolutely not what happened. We did not go to therapy. Neither of us currently keeps a journal. And if anyone had told me we'd be dabbling in "conscious uncoupling" I would've made a barf motion, but that's what we sort of accidentally did. Mostly, we were lazy. Do you know what's easier and cheaper than packing all your shit and moving to another house? Not doing that. We stumbled ass-backward into it, without a plan, barely talked about it, and it still worked, proving that it isn't always hard.

Anyone who has ever dared to share an unconventional idea knows people love to shit all over it. They'll toss out a thousand reasons why what we're doing won't work for them (or anyone). It works for us, for now, which leads me to believe it might work for a few others. I know this because people tell me they want to try it, have tried it, or want to at least propose it to their partner. I know other people who have done it, long before us. And that proves people should stop making perfect the enemy of good. Do I want to live in our current arrangement forever? I most certainly do not. Would we be living together if we didn't have kids? That would be a hard no. This is where we have found ourselves and this is what we have chosen to do given the circumstances. It is choosing us over others' opinions of us. It is choosing to do what feels right, right now, and worrying less about what the typical divorce script looks like or what the future might hold. As it turned out, it was the perfect year to give up thinking about the future entirely. Expectations—in marriage, in life, about what we are owed, about what we can control—have always been the problem.

But I don't need to convince you. I don't need to convince anyone. The only people I've cared about throughout all of this are the four who are still currently living in this house, including me. At the end of the day, I believe the same thing about divorce that I believe about abortion: If you don't like it, don't get one.

I wrote this book in reverse order, starting from where I stood. That part felt easy at first, because my thinking was current, my perspective inseparable from my experience. But I knew I needed to reach back, much further back. But in reaching back I was still seeing everything through my current lens. I couldn't really remember how I thought or felt twenty or thirty years ago. So I sifted through old yearbooks and letters, a pile of high school and college journals I hadn't even remembered (I thought it would be just a few, it was more like twenty), and even some high school and college class assignments. It's impossible to reconstruct roughly thirty-five or so years of my romantic relationship history and, besides, this book isn't intended to be a play-by-play of my life. I am not famous and that would be boring. Mostly I was looking for clues. I was looking for the aha moments that would make it all seem so plain. I discovered quite a few, but not the ones I expected.

This book is for the ambivalent, for the second-guessers and overthinkers, for anyone who has ever felt alone in their marriage and been told, "It's not so bad, what are you complaining about?" And it's for anyone who feels like *what was even the fucking point* of that relationship, that marriage, or my entire life while we're at it?

The point is, if you look deeply enough, behind you, all around you, you might find the mistakes weren't as colossal as you believed. What if you did get smarter over time and what if you weren't all that dumb to begin with? What if you experienced more moments of grace than you realized? What if you knew yourself better when you were a teenager than you thought you did? And what if you discovered all the ways you rationalized changing yourself over time because you thought that would make you a better person but, instead, all those changes just made you less *you*?

You might be a little less hard on yourself in some ways and much harder on yourself in others. You might discover that, surprise, surprise, cis-het marriage is an outdated and often unequal arrangement that we keep clinging to because it's what everyone else is doing so why not? We haven't evolved nearly as much as we like to think we have. And you might discover that divorce has been imbued with feelings of such darkness and shame that rarely does anyone question whether it can be handled differently. We just get ready to fight and prepare to lose.

Ultimately, every marriage is a story written by two people and retold, with varying degrees of accuracy and all sorts of hidden agendas, by everyone around them—their children, their families and friends, acquaintances, strangers. When there is a writer in a marriage, there is an unfair advantage. Because that version (this version) will be the only version recorded, as if it is the one true version. I am here to tell you it is not. I have done my level best to be careful and fair while portraying my experiences honestly, sometimes darkly, other times perhaps a little too cavalierly.

The most important keepers of this marriage story—Jon and our children—initially reviewed the essays that pertained most directly to them. Jon went on to read the full manuscript several times, only requesting minor adjustments. He never once asked me to take anything out, an act of unfathomable openness and generosity for someone so private.

Memory is fallible and perspective inherently biased. I have reconstructed details and dialogue to the best of my ability. Some names have been changed and identifying details altered or omitted where appropriate. This is not a court document. This is a love story. It is, as many marriages tend to be, the story of one's life.

Prologue: The Honeymoon

I am writing you from my honeymoon.

The honeymoon of my divorce.

I am not on a beach or holding a coconut pierced with a straw. I am not on a plane to anywhere. I am not walking a cobblestone path to a quaint pub, teetering in my impractical honeymoon shoes. I am not backpacking nor road-tripping. I am not filled with blind hope. I am not divorced, not yet.

What I am is free.

I am free from a yearslong conversation about how happy is happy enough? I have continuously asked myself how I could possibly be so selfish as to prioritize my own happiness. Isn't it incredible what marriage and motherhood will do to your most basic sense of what you deserve?

On the ledger we all keep, tallying our misery and joy, or weighing the tediousness of thankless tasks against the appreciation that another person knows all of our faults and elects to stay anyway, I am constantly recalculating:

+ He is a good father. A strong, warm, involved one. A father who does more than almost any other man I know. That kind of father.

- I have no regrets (yet). Will leaving (or staying) be one of them?

+ Our kids.

- I am one good, or possibly bad, offer away from having an affair and have been for some time now. Where is everyone? I thought that part would be easy.

+ He cleaned and decorated the house for my birthday and ordered my favorite cake from the best bakery in town, even though three weeks from that date we would be telling our kids we were separating. Even though we had agreed a year before to get a divorce. He wrote me a thoughtful card, even with everything that was unraveling between us.

- He is not curious about my work, I am not curious about his. In general, we stopped asking each other how we were, what we thought, and what we wanted a long time ago. We stopped being curious about each other, period. You cannot spend your life with someone without curiosity. It is as devastating as infidelity, yet somehow working in a slower, gentler, more insidious way. It is being unfaithful to your own life.

+ He is kind. He is a good man. These two realities kept us married twice as long as they should have. Because the message I've internalized since the beginning of our relationship is that I am a bitch and he is a gem. I am lucky. I am the only one who is lucky here. I will clearly never get this lucky again. I already have more than I deserve.

- He does not talk, which is a sweeping generalization. Of course he *talks*. He talks and is gregarious in a crowd. Slap your back, get you a drink, give you a big strong hug, and cook a meal with and for you. For over twenty years I mistook these actions as a form of reflection and connection. For over twenty years I have essentially been having circular arguments with myself where I posit a problem, weigh the pros and cons aloud, and come to a conclusion. All on my own. He is often there only as an audience.

+ At my lowest and most anxiety-filled, he will tell me he believes in me. He tells me I can do it, I can do anything. I have grown accustomed to this. He has carved out a pool of empathy in the world only for me. A pool I am able to wade through whenever I need it.

+ I trust him with my life.

+ We are good partners in just about every way that doesn't include marriage, which I understand sounds ridiculous. Being there for our kids, taking care of our house, throwing fun parties, tackling mundane shit, and sticking together when life or the world gets especially rough. Not bad for two people who mostly just text each other about what to pick up at the market.

- I want to be alone.

+ But what if I'm alone forever?

- But I just said that's what I wanted? I can't imagine doing this again, this whole relationship thing, this whole marriage thing. But isn't that exactly the type of sentiment the Vows section of the *New York Times* is littered with?

- I don't think I care about being alone forever.

+ But the devil you know, et cetera and so forth.

Here I am, adding, subtracting, and checking our balance. But he is handsome, but he is good, but he is imperfect. And why is it only about him anyway? There are two people in this relationship. When have I not been there for him? What have I not asked? What have I not done? What have I missed? How does my ledger look? And, honestly, do I even care?

I am so tired of questions.

I am so tired of wanting to want to make it work.

What do you do when there is no drama? There is no screaming or phone-throwing. Not much fighting at all, come to think of it. No one was fucking someone they shouldn't. Hell, no one was fucking someone they should. It was not miserable. It was not wonderful. Well, it was wonderful once. But now it just . . . is.

I do not have an ex-husband. We do not even live in separate houses, not yet. We are still sleeping in the same bed for God's sake. We still parent our kids together. He makes dinner every night and I decide whether to join him. We are roommates. Which is what we were before, but now everyone knows. We attend school events together and go to friends' parties. I am no longer wearing my ring. He is still wearing his. It is not because he is in love with me, nor is he heartbroken. He doesn't like change and I have been chasing it.

When I was in my twenties I thought I knew everything about everyone. I thought I knew myself. And I certainly thought I knew what was going on in the romantic relationships around me. Just as no one can truly know what has gone on in my marriage other than Jon and me, I can't begin to fathom what is happening in anyone else's. I thought I knew who would last (and is "lasting" even the point?). I thought it would be easy (it was so easy in the beginning). I thought if your marriage was hard that just meant you didn't love each other enough (who knows, maybe it does?). I thought there could be nothing worse than divorce.

Even though I thought I was more than ready, when I finally slipped off my ring and wiggled it into the velvet slit of a ring box, I was indescribably sad. I had just turned fifty. I was a cliché. I thought, *the first person to refer to me as "a woman in transition" is getting a knuckle punch to the nipple.*

I tell anyone who will listen I am not worried about a man who has a full head of hair and a smashing smile, who would never hurt the proverbial fly, who is actually handy for a living and loves to cook. I am not worried about that man finding another partner. He will do just fine. He will probably trip and fall backward into a fresh thirty-year-old vagina. But what about *me*? Then I pause and think, *excuse me ma'am, what exactly do you mean by "what" "about" "me"?*

So I write you now from this honeymoon, and this is all I know for sure:

It was not my fault.

It was not his fault.

It was my fault.

It was his fault.

It was the fault of two people who believed in marriage but had little idea what they were in for. Which, come to think of it, is true of most everyone. I didn't know myself. He didn't know himself. We didn't know each other. Unbelievably, startingly, this is the truth.

And, somehow, twenty-five years later, it still is.

And, somehow, it still worked for a long time anyway.

I have come to this understanding: None of us will ever truly know the people we think we know so well. Our best friends. Our siblings. Our parents. Our partners. People are fundamentally unknowable. Even our children, people we have made. When all is said and done, we tell ourselves a story about who we think we are. We tell ourselves a story about who we think other people are. Their flaws, their motivations, their innermost thoughts and desires. We prefer our versions. We *understand* our versions. But all that aside, what we all have in common is this:

Please see me, please care about me.

This is what we are mewling into the universe from the minute we are born. From the second we can reach out, swiping the air with a vulnerable open hand, hoping to grasp comfort. Please care about me. Please care *for* me.

Please hold me.

Please love me.

Never leave me.

Why are you leaving me?

I thought marriage was the last place.

Instead it is just one place.

I have no idea what is ahead. I don't know how this book ends. I don't know if by the time I finish writing it we'll be living in separate houses or separate states. Or will we be living upstairs and downstairs from one another, sitting together at meals? Will all four of us still go to Maine in the summer, as we had planned?

I only know what is behind me and smack right in front of me. Nothing has changed and everything has changed. So I write you from this honeymoon, where I feel free. Where, like twenty-five years ago, I have no idea what happens next. I'm no better at predicting my future now than I was back then. I am not here to sob all over these pages; I am (mostly) done with crying. I am here to tell you that divorce, even in its baby stages, is not the worst thing that's ever happened to me.

I'm happy to be here.

ME

Ambition: To go to college, meet and marry the perfect man (but party it up first!), live in Maine, and stay in touch with the best friends I've ever had!

—High school yearbook, 1986

Maiden

It would be odd to begin the story of my marriage without sifting through the years that went into making me, me. I was not born then engaged. I didn't go from the cradle to the altar. I kept my last name, my maiden name, without ever thinking twice about it. I had spent *so long* (it had felt so long, back then) becoming this person. This engaged about-to-be-married person. I had worked so hard to become her, no way was I giving her up that easily. I remember saying half to myself and half to Jon, "Kimberly *Hughes*? I don't even understand who that person *is*. Who is *that*?" It was not a battle. It had never even occurred to him that I might change it.

I thought I was leaving my childhood and adolescence and everything doofy about my life behind when I got married. I thought marriage would make me good and serious. I thought adulthood replaced childhood, and marriage replaced whatever the hell it was that I had been doing, like an upgrade in the machine.

It is not my place to speak to how Jon came to our marriage, his childhood, what he thought marriage would do to or for him. I could probably riff a little on it, but I won't. If I knew how he felt or how he thought, this would be a more balanced book and his name would be on the cover, after mine, in alphabetical order.

Besides, being me has always taken up more than enough of my time and attention. Being me has been both my greatest and dumbest project, like watching a baby discover her own hands repeatedly. Entertaining to watch, as if from outside myself, but also, wow just look at that dummy go.

Marriages are made of people. And whether we like it or not, how we became those people is where our marriages begin.

Say Thank You

Maybe my brain doesn't work correctly. Maybe I retained all the wrong memories from childhood. Maybe that's the problem.

I have managed to forget an entire vacation to Disney World when I was twelve but with crystalline recall I can remember pulling into our driveway when I was around five and seeing one of our Great Danes standing on the roof, wagging his tail, covered in blood. He had gone through our second-story window, on purpose, as he did most things. He seemed pretty happy about it. Forty-five years later I can still feel the sway of the car as it made a right turn onto Sidney Avenue, the headlights sweeping the trees, then our house, then *oh my God*.

Even after we moved far from that house I returned often to Rhode Island, staying with my grandparents who lived next door and palling around with my best friend, Maria, who lived one street over. We'd go swimming in the ocean with no supervision whatsoever, not even a teenage lifeguard. Without warning one of us would pretend to be jerked under the water, like in *Jaws*. The other would giggle nervously and yell stuff like "cut it out!" while her mind raced, *what if this was a girl who cried wolf situation? What if there really were great whites in Greenwich Bay?*

When I would be down at the beach alone I'd capture baby jellyfish in a jar and bring them home. I'd sit and stare at them, pondering how neatly they had been designed. They hid nothing. I would watch their little urgent bodies propelling through the salt water until they inevitably died, becoming still flat circles.

I built my personal mythology on vivid details like these—moments of horror, grim comedy, beauty I was convinced existed only for my eyes—and seem to have forgotten much of what happened between those extremes.

One summer, the peak *Jaws* reenactment summer probably, Skylab was falling back to Earth. The thing was, Skylab wasn't designed to return to Earth in any sort of controlled or safe fashion. It was just built to become irrelevant. On the day it was in the process of disintegrating and predicted to imprecisely crash back down, Maria and I decided it was the perfect day to walk five miles round trip to get a slice of pizza. We were ten. I spent most of our walk looking down at the grass for small treasures and directly into the sky, awaiting catastrophe.

I felt my job as a child was to be vigilant. I wore old beat-up no-name tennis shoes into the ocean to protect my feet from pinching crabs. On our walks home from the beach or to the store to buy candy I assumed any man driving too slowly intended to kidnap us. And as we walked alongside a busy road to get pizza, I thought I would be capable of getting out of the way of a 77-ton piece of space trash disintegrating through our atmosphere.

It's never too early to believe in your ability to control absolutely everything.

I was left alone from a shockingly early age and nothing bad happened because of it. I didn't hurt myself or burn the house down. No one molested me. I was a quiet, responsible, independent kid. A moment stands out to me now, maybe I was seven or nine and quite shy, and I was introduced to someone in my father's office. I think this person had either said something nice or given me a piece of candy and I said nothing. And my father, a little embarrassed, said, "Say *thank you.*" I remember thinking, but you never *taught me* to say thank you.

It was as if my parents just expected me to know things.

And eventually I learned some things.

We moved for my father's job twice, from Rhode Island to Wisconsin for a year, then finally settled in the western Massachusetts town where I'd start third grade and eventually graduate from high school.

My memories of Wisconsin are few. I have a brief flash of my first day as the new kid in school, standing out on the playground completely alone. I don't remember anything else about school that year, not my teachers nor any friends I might have made. But I must've made some because I know we rode bikes together and stole milk crates from the alley behind the grocery store. I remember tornado sirens and one beautiful, catastrophic ice storm that knocked the power out long enough to kill all the expensive fish in my dad's saltwater tank.

I remember biting into a tomato thinking for some reason it would taste like an apple and that ruined tomatoes for me for years. I remember smelling a tuna fish sandwich and throwing up. I remember that an elderly woman died on a street corner in downtown Marshall, but I don't remember whether she fell or was hit by a car. I did not know her, and this was not a death I witnessed firsthand. But I found myself at that intersection shortly after it happened and couldn't stop staring at the stain where her blood had seeped into the concrete. A woman had been here. This is where her head hit the sidewalk. And now she was gone. Even after the blood washed away, I was never able to stand at that spot without thinking about how it had pooled there.

Our house had a sunken living room with lights sunk into the ceiling. It felt like the glamorous future compared to our two-story cottage in Rhode Island. For a time my aunt Janet, with her long straight sheet of sandy brown hair, lived with us, too. She also seemed like the glamorous future. She would go on to hitchhike up Big Sur and live in Aspen. She once met John Denver when she worked at the Aspen airport before Aspen was a big deal and it's her I think of whenever I hear "Rocky Mountain High." I remember her being asked if she was dating anyone; my grandparents seemed to be especially preoccupied with whether or not she would ever get married at the rate she was going. But to me, her life seemed exciting. Her life seemed like freedom.

Monson is a small town in western Massachusetts that was founded in 1760 when people got tired of traveling over hills to Brimfield. That attitude feels fitting. It was originally home to granite quarries, a hat factory, and woolen and cotton mills. But by the time we moved there, all of that was long gone and had been replaced by plastics factories and Zero Manufacturing. I was led to believe Zero made toilet seats and only now am I questioning whether that was a rural legend. In a bit of cultural foreshadowing, Dan Wesson Arms manufactured revolvers in a former school building at the edge of town. Tambrands, the maker of Tampax, was located in the next town over and some of my classmates would go on to work there when we were in high school and during summer breaks from college. My town was a real firepower and pussies type of place, awash in maturity and sophisticated jokes, as you might be able to tell.

Summers in a small town buried in the woods were of course different than those spent near the ocean. We had a bug zapper that attracted a Las Vegas–showgirl array of moths that would linger on the trees long after the sun came up. Grand Luna moths with translucent lime-green wings. Small white moths that looked like they were sporting ermine coats. I would coax them onto my finger and stare at their crabby expressions. Rosy maple moths striped hot pink and bright yellow, very '80s.

I'd play *Charlie's Angels* with my best friend next door and if I didn't get to be Jill then I would simply go home. I'd meander around the woods picking wild blueberries or digging into the dirt with my bare hands looking for arrowheads, any triangular-shaped rock would do. By the time I was a teenager I'd often eat dinner alone in my room, watching my little black-and-white TV.

My mother bred and showed Great Danes, so she was away at dog shows most weekends. My dad and I would spend most Saturday mornings washing his car then go out for donuts. Or we'd play catch or T-ball in our yard and end up at the mall at some point, getting slices of cheese pizza. We saw some pretty girls walk by on one of those trips and as we munched on pizza he said, "One day you're going to be a knockout just like them" and I thought, *yes, I think I should be.* I was likely wearing Toughskins and a western shirt, had buck teeth and a Kristy McNichol haircut and probably hadn't bathed in a week, and still I thought, *yes, that sounds about right.*

I had always assumed I would be famous and spent a great deal of time draping sheets around me to replicate evening gowns. I would stay up late and watch *The Tonight Show Starring Johnny Carson* and feel like sitting on that couch was my destiny.

It's never too early to believe you deserve the world's attention simply for being you.

I rarely heard my parents fight, but I also didn't think of them as being in love or even being friends. They seemed to be bloodlessly ticking through a list of life tasks with almost no emotion to show for the process or one another. They had married only a couple years out of high school and I was born shortly thereafter. Needless to say, those were terrible ideas. Although, let me state for the record, I am grateful to exist.

My parents threw exactly one Christmas party in that house. I can picture a punch bowl and our house uncharacteristically packed and abuzz with neighbors. It felt like not long after that party the neighborhood divorces began. The dads moved out. The dads always moved out.

Once I hit puberty and my parents started what felt like an endless process of separating and getting back together then finally divorcing, if there was genuine or positive attention paid to me by them I didn't feel it. If they ever worried about me, I'm not sure it registered. If there was curiosity about where I was or who I was with, or even just what I was thinking, it rarely landed. I could do just about anything and I did. I never got caught for most of the things I did (at least within a time frame when it would have mattered) and I got falsely accused of things I hadn't done at all.

During one of their early separations I visited my dad at his Sad Separated Dad apartment where there were spider plants, boxes of Lucky Charms I could dig the marshmallows out of without getting in trouble, and a roommate who had been through the Vietnam War. Somewhere I have photos of me playing in the snow and sledding there, but I don't remember much else about it other than I'm pretty sure the entire place was brown. Everything about it felt like failure.

I saw my father cry exactly once, when my parents sat me down and told me they were getting a divorce. Finally. I was older then, a teenager. And although I can still remember every detail about that living room in that moment and where we each sat, I can't remember anything about how I reacted. I don't be-

lieve I cried. I don't think I said much of anything. I think I just
shut down. And my father cried and then he left and then honestly, there you go. I don't remember either of them ever asking
me how I felt or if I had any questions or if they could help me
through this break in our family. They just did what they did
and that was that. I never pined for them to get back together
because they never seemed like they were together in the first
place.

We had been just three people—then two, after my father
moved out—who resided in the same space but lived independently from one another. I was an easy child but a pissed-off
teenager and I felt I had earned the right (don't we all). I was
already becoming a weed that would always find the crack in
the sidewalk to sprout from, without ever needing to be tended.
Why answer to anybody? What was the point?

I was smart without knowing it and channeled this into being a wiseass at school and with my friends, and secretive and
manipulative with my parents as I hit fifteen. I played to the division between them because they made it so easy. If they were
going to continuously put me in the middle, I was going to play
the middle for all it was worth. My mother threatened to have
my car, a two-tone blue 1979 Mercury Monarch my father had
bought for me, taken away. I responded, "Good luck with that.
Like Dad is going to listen to you."

It was easy to pin my bad attitude and burgeoning character
flaws on my parents' divorce. It was the easiest thing in the world.
Every divorce article I would go on to read supported this, as
did every grave conversation I overheard between adults as they
talked about other people's divorces. *What about the children?*
Divorce—a legal dissolution by a court—was a convenient repos-
itory for any and all struggles: anger, anxiety, cynicism, lack of

attachment, lack of commitment, lack of being a good person. A real bad-things catch-all. God forbid I was just born to be some kind of mid-tier asshole. God forbid this legal process might've had an emotional silver lining or two for me—a drive to communicate clearly, a desire to find meaning and explanations for why things happen, and a fundamental acceptance early on that most adults don't know what the hell they're doing. God forbid we blame (or credit) the people involved versus the process. Divorce was a convenient and generic brush with which I could negatively paint my life. Nothing and no one would allow me to tether it to anything good. The mere suggestion felt offensive.

To be clear, mine is not a story of trauma and there are no victims here. It is a story of a fairly typical 1970s and 1980s childhood devoid of guardrails and guidance. It is a story of people who made choices when they were young and those choices had consequences for others, specifically for me, that I don't believe were intended but that doesn't make them any less real. I am not unique. I am not a survivor. I am just a person who was shaped by other people's decisions and behavior, as we all are. This is how life works. I was left to figure out things for myself for a long time and I am surprised to realize all these years later I still am.

Is it ever too late to attempt to blame your childhood for absolutely everything?

When I was a kid, my best friend in the neighborhood would sometimes ask if I wished I had a brother or a sister. Being an only child was a bit of an anomaly back then, especially with such young parents. What could possibly be the reason for not having more? I've suspected having me was a mistake or they realized the hard way (as some parents do) they just weren't cut out to be parents. Or perhaps their marriage didn't work right from the start and they knew it.

My answer to her question was I never wished I had a brother or a sister. I liked being alone then and I have craved it since. I sure wasn't sad about having all the Christmas presents to myself. I didn't have anyone snatching food off my plate, "borrowing" my shit, or holding their finger an inch away from my arm in the car while whispering *but I'm not even touching you.*

The only downside I have identified over time is that I am the only one who knows these stories and memories from the inside. Just once I would've loved to be able to turn to someone around my age, someone who grew up in my house with the same parents in the same town at the same time, and be able to say, "Can you believe this shit?" Just once I would've loved to know if someone else who was even a little bit like me would've also been waiting for things to come crashing down. I wonder if they, too, would've believed they could control everything.

I never doubted I was loved. I still don't. I know I am loved. But I'm not sure I ever felt particularly cared for, especially when caring for me felt challenging and when it would've mattered most.

There is a difference.

Gimme the strength to pursue a social life!!! I'm begging to get yelled at for public displays of affection! Oh yeah, my parents got a divorce. I'll be going on a whale watch next Saturday.

—April 14, 1984, 15 years old

What to Expect When You're Expecting to Be a Gen X Girl

Congratulations! You're going to be born in 1968, a year *Smithsonian* magazine called "The Year That Shattered America"! That's good, right? Until 1991, when Douglas Coupland's book *Generation X: Tales for an Accelerated Culture* is published, your generation will be known as the Baby Bust generation. Sorry, but we can't go for that, no (no), no can do.

I suppose your generation could've also been named after Billy Idol's band, Generation X; or Category X, a group characterized as gravitating to big cities and creative work while also being anti-advertising, anti-authority, and anti-brand in Paul Fussell's 1983 book, *Class: A Guide Through the American Status System*. Coupland mentioned both as inspirations for the title of his landmark book but, man, which one was it? What if I told you Billy Idol named *his* band after another book titled *Generation X*, by Charles Hamblett and Jane Deverson that was published in 1964? This is the kind of circle jerk argument full of deep-cut cultural references you can expect to have for the rest of your miserable life.

Anyway, when your time finally comes at least your generation will be named after something musical and triply literary and don't think you won't shove that down other generations' throats every chance you get. What are they named after? Just some letter that comes after X in the alphabet? Wow, *I'm so sure.*

Year 0–2

Minimum safety standards for child car seats won't be established until the 1970s so good luck to you! You will be left to roll about in a tiny death chair accessorized with a dodgy buckle and flaccid strap. Or someone—a parent, a neighbor, a stranger, honestly who knows—will just hold you on their lap, which will seem overprotective compared to what's going on with your older siblings. They'll just be bouncing around loose in the back of a pickup truck or sitting in the wayback of the family station wagon giving the finger to passing motorists. This illusion of safety wrapped in almost certain death is your generation's Beatles.

Year 3–5

In 1967, nearly half of all mothers stayed home and that proportion will steadily decline over the next two decades. Which means you, small preschool child, will be parented by the first big wave of "Ha ha, *fuck this!*" moms who headed off to work thus bestowing upon you immediate independence, Olympian levels of self-soothing, and a cursory knowledge of first aid. You will spend these early years in nursery school not at all being set on a path to higher education. What's Harvard? You're four! You'll just chill, be social, and have books read to you, setting you on a lifelong quest for maximum culture with minimal effort.

Year 6–11

You are in elementary school now! You are practically an adult! Yours will be a largely feral existence dotted with occasional check-ins for Little Debbie snack cakes, dinner made from soup mix, and a bath once a fortnight. Your parents will be busy attempting to self-actualize and/or divorce and you'll be busy learning about the alphabet and Watergate from TV. They will never, not once, wonder whether you're hydrated.

You will go to and from school on your own; yes, including walking without any parents whatsoever. You will develop the fine-tuned instincts of a jungle cat. You will probably be beaten up a lot or will beat up others a lot and you know who you're not going to tell? *Adults.* You will go missing for hours on end and it won't even register with your parents that you're gone. They might've had you but that doesn't mean they want to see you.

Frankly, it wouldn't matter if all the adults disappeared from the face of the Earth tomorrow. As long as you've got your friends from the neighborhood and a loose dog, you could still survive with just a pocketknife, a can of Tab stolen from your mom, a lighter, a baseball bat, and a box of Bugles salty snacks.

You will probably see *Grease* when it comes out and, well, you have to. That's your one chance. You will be rewarded mightily by *Grease*, which will feature filthy lyrics like "the chicks'll cream" that you won't understand at all. It will also deliver the most powerful lessons of your Gen X girl life—if you want to get a guy, you'll need to change absolutely everything about yourself, start smoking, and dress like a whore.

Year 12–14

You are twelve now! For Generation X, that is child retirement age. Are you smoking yet? What are you waiting for? An engraved invitation, which is still a thing that exists? Also, MTV has launched and the M actually still stands for something. It's exactly this sort of snotty attitude about "the M still standing for something" that's both your curse and your comfort.

Phones are attached to walls and you can only talk to one person at a time so please enjoy both screaming and hearing "GET OFF THE PHONE" every day of your pubescent life. You should also brace yourself for the social and emotional espionage of calling your top-tier best friend, finding her line busy, then calling your lesser lower-tier best friend, and finding her line busy and knowing in your very soul they're talking to each other. You will be faced with one of your first seemingly insurmountable social, moral, and ethical quandaries—do you attempt an emergency breakthrough? And if you do, what's your lie? And if you do, what will you shout at the same time the operator says "emergency breakthrough" before you hang up?

Anyway, make no mistake, everyone is talking on the phone without you, probably about you, *paranoia the destroyer*, ya spaz.

Year 15–18

Here is what you'll believe:

- The United States is boring
- Wars are in the past
- VCRs, CDs, cable TV, and Atari Asteroids are cutting-edge technology
- Politics is something practically dead people care about
- Blue balls are a medical condition
- John Lennon's murder and the Space Shuttle *Challenger* disaster are pointless tragedies so there probably won't be any more of those

The year you graduate from high school will be the same year *Newsweek* runs a cover story titled "Too Late for Prince Charming?" that will state with incredible hyperbole that single women over forty are more likely to be killed by a terrorist than to find a husband. Righteous! You don't know what hyperbole is exactly, so that will definitely stick!

Yours is the last generation that couldn't wait to get the hell away from your parents and do whatever you wanted as if you hadn't been doing that all along. You'll graduate from high school, you'll hear about Black Monday when you're smoking in the stacks at your college library. You'll drink your way through college and graduate into a recession. But then that book, that Douglas Coupland book, will finally come out and you'll have a handle for all of this. Your generation didn't even have an actual name until you were a legal adult, of voting age, could drive, and be drafted.

Congratulations. Or whatever.

Notes from Family Living Class

January 1986, senior year of high school

Engagement—not a legal contract

Marriage contract—agreement of division of assets at the time of divorce

Engagement period is usually turbulent because "no 2 people agree on everything"

Length of engagement period should be 6 months to one year—no longer than 2 years. Long enough to find out if the relationship is based on similar interests, backgrounds, and attitudes or if the attraction is mostly physical.

During the engagement period sexual pressure is much greater, especially before the marriage.

Recommended to be married for three years before having a child.

Reasons to sometimes wait until 20s to marry:
1. More experiences w/different people
2. Decisions have been made as to how you wish to live
3. Education is complete
4. Career is started

Why do older people (30ish) sometimes have difficulty adjusting to a first marriage? They are set in their ways, they are used to living independently.

Why is it often dangerous to get married during the most romantic part of a relationship? Passion is at the highest point it will *ever* be at in the relationship, once this goes down, disappointment/arguments may set in.

Teenage Dirtbag

I worked in a porn shop the summer between my freshman and sophomore years of college. It was not a desperate choice. It was not a cool girl choice. It wasn't even a rebellious choice. Porn was still secretive, grimy, and a lot harder to get. And I, an eighteen-year-old girl, helped peddle it. It was a job I fell into. It was a job I then spent most of my life trying to forget.

I worked alone in a one-room building on the side of a fairly desolate stretch of nondescript western Massachusetts road, as are most western Massachusetts roads not intended for tourists. Technically it was a two-room building if you counted the tiny bathroom where I would sometimes dye my hair a shade of brown so dark it looked black and blue in direct sunlight.

Only one employee worked there at a time, shockingly we were not a volume business. Each of us was responsible for opening, closing, reshelving videos, and cashing out the register. I still have sweaty nightmares about this job, rooted in my fear of ever having to work retail again or be responsible for a customer service experience of any kind. These nightmares are usually about not understanding how the new cash register works or not being able to get the key in the door at night. I think of these nightmares as proof of how little I reflected on this job or my safety back then.

It was primarily a video rental shop but also offered a smattering of other products like vibrators, edible panties, and a single rack of cheap lingerie. It was located catty-corner from a strip club that would sometimes hold male stripper nights, which were gross indeed, but the bartenders would serve us. I was nothing if not pragmatic.

If you don't know how someone can just "fall into" working in a porn shop, then either you've never lived in a rural town or you were ambitious. Or you had parents who asked questions like, "Where are you working these days?" Or maybe I just lied? Truly I can't remember now. I did lie a lot. And I fell in and out of a lot of things back then. I fell out of the quasi-stoner clique and inexplicably into the lower tier of the jock/cheerleader one. I fell into and out of crushes constantly, like playing the slots, believing eventually one of them has gotta hit. I fell into a surprisingly limited sexual relationship with a thirty-one-year-old man when I was still in high school. His buddy was a cop and certainly knew what was going on. So that whole thing about small towns being salt of the earth, our national moral compass, our best American selves? Get the fuck out of here with that.

I had originally been employed by a general—a "good," a "normal"—video store. It was located in the center of town, not on the outskirts, like most good and normal things are. This was one of only two jobs I've ever been straight-up for-poor-performance fired from. It probably had a little something to do with not understanding nor caring about even the most basic tenets of customer service. I didn't like people impeding on my precious alone time that I was, in fact, not being paid to indulge in. Simply put, I was a typical teenage jerk who didn't even have the good sense to hide it.

One of the managers was a woman in her late twenties, a

stunner with a thick mane of prematurely gray hair, and a magnetic, saucy personality. She decided to open her own video store, an adult one, and asked if I'd be interested in working for her. Given I wasn't working at all I'm pretty sure the intense negotiation process went something like this: I answered the phone. I listened. I shrugged. I said, "okay." And I hung up.

Would I have shrugged and said, "okay" had it been a man opening that adult video store, offering me that job? I'm not sure. But I'm not *not* sure either. I assume I've always been wary of men, but that isn't true at all. I assume I've always been doing the backstroke through a pool of ambition but that came much later. The truth is I was born with a hard, dark lump of laziness where a few of my internal organs should be.

My primary activities that summer, the porn shop summer, were sleeping until noon, Hoovering a bowl of Special K, and driving over to where my friend Linda was house-sitting at one of the few houses in our town with an in-ground pool. We splayed ourselves out, covered in tanning oil, and flipped through *Seventeen* and *People* and *Glamour*. It was very *Fast Times at Ridgemont High* except without the all-the-way sex or abortions. Then I'd get dressed, order takeout from the restaurant across from the shop, and stroll into my job. I went back to college in September the tannest and most relaxed I would ever be.

The following spring, I returned during break to pick up hours. I called UCLA one afternoon from work, using my calling card, to follow up on my transfer application. The woman on the other end of the line said, "You didn't receive a response?" I said, "no" and she replied, "Oh! Well, you've been accepted." I had already decided to leave the state college I was attending, feeling done with whatever it was they were teaching me, and had already been rejected by UC Santa Cruz. I was fully prepared to pump gas in the fall and was surprised to learn that whatever coin toss the UCLA admissions office had executed had worked out in my favor. I would soon be living 2,915 miles away, which seemed like the correct distance.

I spent my work shifts surrounded by empty video sleeves plastered with images of naked women who were buttered up and shiny like brioche, a word I didn't know back then. Now when I see that sort of oily greasiness all I can think is, *good luck getting those stains out of those sheets. Listen to me, you need to pre-treat that right now. And soak them, probably.* I don't think I felt like my sexuality was a part of me then, something that belonged to me and that I could shape however I pleased. It felt like it had to be activated, like an ingredient in someone else's recipe.

My introduction to sexuality and sex was, on the one hand, my mother dropping a copy of a book about sex on my bed and saying, "You might be interested in this," turning on her heel and walking out, and my father saying not a single word about it at all. And then on the other hand, being surrounded by images of women who were bent over or splayed open, displaying their complicated pink crotches like baboons at the zoo. I'm still looking for the middle ground between these extremes—the scintillating and filthy, the acceptable and informational. Or maybe this is still just who I am, perpetually predisposed to ignore the middle.

I accelerated from knowing so little about sex to buying lingerie and vibrators at a discount when I was still a teenager. I understand that in the full, rich range of sexual exploration, turn-ons, and toys, this is embarrassingly vanilla, yet it was certainly sufficient to later plunge me into shame. I was doing a job I had just fallen into, when it felt like no one cared enough to question what I was doing or, alternately, frame it in a way that at least made it feel like a progressive or sex positive choice. It took years before I wanted to see a vibrator or a lacy thing again. I can trace my visceral hatred of the word "panties" to this job. It's a word with the leer built right in.

I never watched the porn in that shop, although, and I'm sure you saw this one coming, one of the most common opening lines from customers as they placed the empty box down on the counter and turned the cover so it faced me was, "So, how is this one?" Always said with a smug grin, perhaps a raised eyebrow. What I wouldn't give now to deliver some bullshit esoteric take on *Backside to the Future* or *Saturday Night Beaver*.

These men could see I had a TV and a VCR right there behind the counter, and in their porn-pickled brains must've assumed I spent my time watching and personally rating all the porn while wearing no pants. When in reality, the takeout lunch I had picked up, a burger and fries encased in a sweaty Styrofoam clamshell, grew cold and soggy on top of the TV as I fetched their tapes. And what I was actually watching were videos from the other store, the store I had been fired from, the "good" video store. *Top Gun*, *Pretty in Pink*, *St. Elmo's Fire*, *The Breakfast Club*, that sort of shit.

"I wouldn't know. I don't watch these." I don't remember what I said. Maybe I said nothing and just met them with my burgeoning dead eyes. Like *just give me your fucking membership number, asshole*. And don't hand me the card, put it down on the counter and slide it across. Like I'm going to touch *that*.

Two decades later, I was visiting a high school classmate's parents with my family in tow. His father trained his eyes on me, lowered his voice, and as if to make a point he asked, in front of my husband and infant son, "Didn't you used to work at that . . . video store?" while his wife was sliding muffins out of the oven. He let the question hang in the air, not once averting his eyes. The question managed to be both sleazy and accusatory. I imagined for a moment that he must've wondered how I, a wayward slut and former porn peddler, had managed to have such a good and clean family. Such a *normal* life. Had I deserved it? By then I was deeply familiar with the way boys and men could judge and punish girls and women for not sticking to the path.

I matched his stare as I held my son close and replied, "Yes. I did."

The muffins were delicious.

These Are the Things I
Know about Myself

May 12, 1991, 22 years old

I'm selfish

I wish I was Madonna

I almost enjoy fighting

I've talked to the mirror since I was little because I've always
    believed I would be famous

I get even with people who have fucked with me

I don't want to get old

I like sleeping in the nude

I'm obsessed with my image

There's an innate goodness about me

I'm a bitch

I have a side that's very manipulative, scheming, intelligent

I say I want intimacy but I'm not sure what that is

I use people because I feel that they couldn't care enough about
    me to be hurt

When someone rejects me I believe they, deep down, are in love
    with me

The people around me decide my morals

I love sex, I love talking about sex, I love thinking about sex, I
    love having sex

I'm not tolerant of people

A lot of people can't deal with me but they do because of who I am

I wouldn't want to be treated the way that I treat some people

I have no idea where I'll be in five years

I'll be successful

My father controls me more than he knows

I don't know anything, really, about my parents

I wish I was a man, sometimes

I wonder what my life would be like if I had a sister or a brother

I am too often the center of my universe

I'm fascinated by the negative

Sometimes I feel like a cartoon

I think people envy me for negative reasons

I'm insanely independent

It's difficult for me to be affectionate

I need to document everything about my life—writing, photographs, tapes

I have to have my way

MARRIAGE

When will I meet the man that I will fall in love with?

Will I ever?

I wonder, if and when I do meet him, who he will be. What will he look like and what will his voice sound like. I wonder where he is now and what his life is like. Does he need someone also? Is he younger or older than me? What is his name? How will we meet?

—December 6, 1988, 20 years old

A Relationship History, in Brief

Before I met Jon the longest relationship I had ever had lasted three months.

A Portrait of the Man and the Moment

The man I would go on to marry didn't look like the man I would go on to marry when I met him. He had hair down to his ass, a questionable facial hair configuration, and although he was only twenty-five, all that hair combined to make him look like a weed dealer in his forties.

I lived in Portland, Oregon, by then and none of those details made him stand out. I had attempted to move from LA to Seattle after the Northridge earthquake but the friends-of-friends who promised to put me up in Seattle told me when I arrived that, actually, I couldn't stay there after that night. I was trying not to panic, but as I watched the Academy Awards from their couch I kept thinking, *no one in LA would tell you they were kicking you out on Oscar night.* My next thought was, *you know what, I already hate this place.* The next morning I repacked my car, retrieved my dog, Lula, from the kennel, and drove back down to Portland.

I had originally stopped in Portland on my way up to Seattle, staying with other, better friends-of-friends. When I returned they took me on as a project and toured me through different neighborhoods. They let my dog stay in their house even though she had split her tail open by whacking it hard against door jambs. When she wagged, her blood spattered across walls and our shins, a happy horror.

Hopefully, just once in your life, you will find a place where you feel like you belong. It will feel effortless and you will barely be able to grasp your good fortune. Portland was that place for me. I spent every waking minute of my life in Los Angeles wishing I were taller, thinner, had bigger tits, smaller hips. I wished my hair was straighter and blonder and lifted just so in the sun. I wished I was as gorgeous and genetically interchangeable as seemingly every woman around me. I wanted to be a different human creature entirely, like the girls who lived across from me and my roommates. They would study out on their deck wearing bikinis as if that was normal, while I sat inside my apartment gaining weight, smoking cigarettes, and glowering at them. But in Portland there were women of all shapes and sizes, hair colors and cuts, fire and fluidity. There were few bikinis, which is to be expected in a place where it rains half the year. *My kind of place.* I could be anyone I wanted to be there. I could even be me.

I eventually found a small apartment in a big house, no roommates. I vowed never another roommate after tallying over forty between college dorms, one summer flophouse on Cape Cod, and several post-college apartments and houses. I applied to the one temp agency that funneled temps to the one advertising agency where I wanted to work, Wieden+Kennedy, Nike's ad agency. My money was quickly draining down and the same day I called to find out how much I could make selling my blood plasma, I got a call for a gig as a temp copy typist and receptionist at W+K. I said to myself, *you, young lady, may retain your plasma.*

I don't remember the first time I met Jon, specifically. It was a time and a place where we'd leave work and rove the city in packs, to Rialto, a pool hall and off-track betting parlor one block over from our office; or to Monte Carlo, an Italian American restaurant in SE that hosted disco nights on Fridays; or to any of a number of strip clubs, bars high and low, and what felt like a hundred different venues where we would go see bands.

While I had navigated my way to Portland and Wieden+ Kennedy through a series of zigs and zags fueled by ambition and disasters both natural and man-made, Jon's sister, who also worked at W+K, had secured his freelance production assistant job for him. He had made a good friend there and that good friend shared an office with a good friend I had made. So we overlapped in spaces like that and we overlapped in group outings that were, without exception, fueled by alcohol.

On one particular night, a grab bag of creatives, print production managers, account people, and Jon and I sloshed around town from bar to bar. He had had too much to drink and was slurry and touchy, not in a threatening way but in a way I did not want to deal with at all. The merciless boys I grew up with ridiculed anyone who behaved like a sloppy drunk and this was now my lifelong legacy. I had retained their disdain for such behavior while acquiring the social survival skill of appearing coherent and soberish even when I was quasi-blackout drunk.

One of my friends became interested in Jon that night, due not only to his handsome face, nice smile, and broad shoulders but also to his forceful shoulder and back-of-the-neck massages delivered with his big mitts. That all does combine to have a certain effect. She asked me if she could have him, as if he were a doll or a book, and I was like, "Oh you can have him alright." But she didn't and I didn't and we all moved on with our lives for a few weeks.

When I returned from back East, a trip that had taken me to my hometown on the 4th of July and my grandparents' 50th wedding anniversary dinner, the kind of vacation that returns you to yourself but also makes you just as happy to leave, I also returned to a buzz in the office. *Did you see Jon? Did you see his haircut? Holy cow he looks like Brandon Walsh. You've gotta see him* pinged down the hallways, up and down the stairs, and at the coffee shop across the street. He no longer worked at W+K, his gig only lasting three months. I didn't know he had stopped by the office that day just for me.

I was a platinum blonde then, a Hole-era Miss World wannabe, having already developed a taste for drastic changes and big reveals at parties after less than a year in Portland. Three months earlier I had spent five hours before a work party getting my hair stripped of all its color and dyed, resulting in a schedule of upkeep and ongoing expense that were the equivalent of owning an exotic pet.

I had also finally been hired full-time as a print traffic manager, which one would assume involves cars (my perpetually confused family's favorite joke!) but instead meant I was responsible for shuttling print ads through the creative and production process. I was in the reprint room, where copies of completed print ads were stored, when Jon stopped by. I was either pulling or filing reprints when I heard a man say, "Hi." And, yes, fine, his haircut looked exactly like Brandon Walsh's but his face, his suddenly bare face, looked like a young Russell Crowe's and I wish people would keep their early '90s handsome men references straight. He smiled at me from one side of a towering set of metal shelves stacked with reprints and I smiled from the other.

I had seen a lot of smiles on a lot of men's faces by that point in my life and many of them could best be described as "on the make" smiles. But his smile was different. It was warm and open and dazzling. Now clean-shaven, I could see his cleft chin, just like a movie star's. His now-short hair was already going gray and contained a cowlick so stubborn it would one day prevent our daughter from having the bangs she so desperately wanted.

He asked me out on a date.

I said yes.

He showed up on time.

When you have spent your life waiting for people to show up for you, the impact of him simply showing up, and showing up on time no less, cannot be overstated. It was the first of what would be thousands of gestures that altered the trajectory of my emotional life. It was the first time I realized I could and should expect more.

That's not to say our first date progressed in a way that led me to believe we had a future. It was awash in red flags, but red flags are like passages in the Bible: you can pluck them out of context and bend them to suit the story you wish to tell.

When he had offered to pick up drinks to bring to the small party where our date would begin, I assumed he'd bring a bottle of wine or perhaps a six-pack of good beer. But instead he showed up with a bottle of Jack Daniel's, and a six-pack of Coke. He was still unemployed. He smoked weed in the car between our destinations (I didn't smoke weed, at all). Those red flags fooled me into thinking this (motions around) *whole thing* was obviously going nowhere. I decided, *you know what, I'm not only going to break lady code and eat on this date, I'm going to Convenience Store Eat.* As in, "pull over at this Plaid Pantry so I can get a full-size bag of sour cream and onion chips and a liter of Diet Coke and I am going to eat all of that in your car right now." And, really, once you break that code you might as well just go ahead and break the rest of them.

We kissed in front of his friends, friends I had only just met that night. At the club where we went to see Peter Murphy from

Bauhaus, a singer and a band I knew not at all, I thought, *sure I'll drink this Long Island iced tea your friend the bartender made that's so strong it tastes like lighter fluid.* And I decided to take that night—the party and his friends, the rock star and that show, another bar and his friend's band—for all the fleeting and temporary good times I thought they were. Like, sure we can go to my apartment at the end of the night, or more accurately very early the next morning, on our first (and clearly only) date. And sure you don't have to leave and sure, sure, sure. Let's do whatever. Carpe dum-dum, who cares.

So profound was my singleness at the time that I slept in a twin bed. Twin beds are for children and prisoners. So Jon and I ended up falling asleep on the floor, the only surface with room enough for both of us, half our clothes scattered all around us like a halo the next morning.

Inexplicably, we went on more dates. I experienced the extreme discomfort of being in work meetings with his sister who would brightly ask, "So, did you have a good time with my brother last night?" We went for a weekend away with his friends, watched hydroplane races and played pickleball during the day, and had sex for the first time in his friend's mother's bed (to be clear, she was not in it). Within weeks Jon had unofficially moved into my apartment, through the sheer force of his constant presence and attention, warmth and flexibility. Apparently it was an option to not play games. Apparently it was possible to just be on the same side. Apparently you could fall in love, just like that. Eventually we moved next door together, into a bigger apartment and a bigger bed.

From the minute I had rolled back into Portland every single aspect of my life had snapped into place. Sometimes you get so used to things being hard or just not working out that you don't know what to do with yourself when they're easy. But, just in case, there will be a random acquaintance or coworker or member of your own family around to tell you how *lucky* you are. Just in case you thought you deserved happiness and joy and the love of a good person. Just so you can, for the rest of your life, have this small yet nagging sense that maybe you didn't deserve them. Or him. Or anything. That it was all just big dumb random luck.

This is what I remember about being in love with Jon:

I remember the way to my heart was paved with flowers stolen from weddings, hotel lobbies, and our neighbor's hydrangea bushes. I remember sitting on the couch in my first Portland apartment, probably wearing only an oversize T-shirt and underpants, and him turning around and looking at me from the kitchen, welling up with tears. He was so happy. I had never experienced anyone feeling so happy about me at the same time I felt so happy about them. I had never felt adored by a man, not like this. I thought I would always have to trick one of them into liking me or at least give them enough to drink until they thought they might.

Within weeks we said to each other, *you know what? I didn't see myself ever getting married but I could see myself marrying you.* Within weeks I found myself thinking, *I bet he would make a great father.* Within three months we had told each other *I love you*, something I had never said to anyone I wasn't related to. It was a sure and certain feeling, unshakable. I had been looking for this feeling and trying to imagine this feeling for what seemed like my entire life.

I was never one of those girls who thought boys were gross. I shared graham crackers with a boy in nursery school and, bam, instant boyfriend. If you wanted to play some sort of doctor-patient/person-tied-to-the-train-tracks/cops-and-robbers game I was always, always up for it. I would definitely come up with some imaginary ropes that needed to be loosened or pretend injuries that needed to be tended to that were always suspiciously located right around my crotch area. I had always been boy crazy. But boys were in my past now. Here was a man. And here was our moment.

We were a certain age (he was 25, I was 27). I was finally on The Path. His friends were getting married. My friends were getting married. And now we had friends we could refer to as *our* friends and guess what? They were getting married, too.

We took a vacation together the following summer, after we had been dating for a year. We drove up and down and all over the East Coast. He met my family and I met his extended family who he hadn't seen since he was a teenager. After he met my mother for the first time, along with my grandparents, aunt and uncle and cousins, he turned to me in the car and said, "You know she doesn't listen to you, right?" and I was like, "*What?*"

We camped alone in Maine, on the same beach where three generations of my family had vacationed, and I waited impatiently for the marriage proposal that surely must be coming. This was how the narrative arc worked.

But it didn't come.

I was mad (disappointed, hurt) but it didn't last. We drove to Massachusetts and attended my 10th high school reunion where all my friends realized they preferred Jon to me. Who could blame them? Who else would meet these jackasses, jackasses who tested the boundaries of his good nature, then respond, "Wow your friends are really funny"? It was the first time I paused and thought, *wait a minute, are they?* Aren't everyone's high school friends like this? Or is this just a Massachusetts thing?

We returned to Portland and our simple, easy lives. Working, going out, sleeping, watching TV, having sex, drinking coffee, on repeat. On Saturdays we drifted in and out of record stores and thrift shops and took hangover-reversing naps in the late afternoon then went out again on Saturday night and did the same stuff all over again on Sunday.

On one of our Saturday excursions, undoubtedly after having slept in until 11 a.m. or some other ridiculous hour enjoyed by the young and child-free, we browsed through a vintage store. I looked in the jewelry case for aurora borealis bracelets and gumball-size cocktail rings set with citrine and instead spied a diamond engagement ring. While Jon was in another part of the store, I looked back over my shoulder then asked to try it on. It was simple, beautiful, and subtle. It slid easily onto my finger.

When he walked over to see what I was up to I held up my left hand and said, "Look, it fits!" as if that's why anyone buys an engagement ring.

We left the store without the ring, but I couldn't stop thinking about it. It fitting was a sign, I was convinced. And it was cheap, relatively speaking, I think about $250. I floated the idea of getting it, suggesting splitting the cost, because this was just how modern and different and *special* we were going to be. I was making more money than he was and wasn't it silly and more than a little outdated for a man to spend a bunch of money on a ring he wasn't even going to wear? We were going to do marriage better than anyone else, everyone would see. But first we would have to, you know, get engaged.

Eventually we went back to that shop and we bought that engagement ring together. Jon placed the ring box on the shelf above our kitchen sink and that's where it sat. I would wash dishes by hand and it was there. We would make a meal together and it was there. I would make coffee, he would slice tomatoes, I would write at the kitchen table, he would sweep the kitchen floor, and still it was there. We went to bed, we woke up, and every free moment in between there it sat. And every moment it sat there, I stared at Jon.

"What?"

"You know what."

When he finally proposed, and by "finally" I'm talking a week or two after we bought the ring together, I actually responded, "Really, do you mean it?!" as if I hadn't been mentally grinding him down every waking minute of his life since we walked out of that store. As if I hadn't been trying to beam directly into his brain, "I found the ring, we bought it together, holy shit can you please just do the other part already?"

For years afterward when someone would cheerfully ask, "How did he propose??" I would transform the details of my mental coercion into a funny story or I would change the subject.

Before we called our family and friends to share our news I said, "We should have some idea of the date, even just a ballpark, because people will ask." We couldn't choose September 17th because that was my parent's wedding date. Obviously the success or failure of a marriage is largely predicated on whether or not you've jinxed yourself with arbitrary details such as these. We settled on October.

When we told one of Jon's closest friends, who was two weeks away from his own wedding, he jokingly responded, "Sucker." It became an inside joke throughout our marriage, a wiseass response to other people's good news; initially engagement news, then eventually pregnancy news. That couple, the "sucker" couple, divorced.

We invited our friends to join us for a beer or five at Barley Mill Pub, just down the street from our apartment. We practically skipped there, a bit tipsy from champagne, a lot happy from everything else, and rushed to tell each other things we hadn't already shared. It all tumbled out like a pile of historical puppies.

Before everyone arrived I decided to tell him which men might be invited to our wedding who I had previously slept with because, well, there would be a few. He didn't flinch. His future wife, fucking other people, a concept that didn't seem to bother him at all. Meanwhile, I absolutely did not want to hear about his one long-term girlfriend, no thank you. As far as I was concerned, his life had started right then, with me.

Of course his life hadn't started with me, though. It had started in Alaska, in a stable and loving home in a textbook nuclear family, a mom, a dad, a sister, two cats. I never heard him say a negative word about his parents, a concept I couldn't remotely wrap my head around. Every photo of him and his sister together showed them hugging each other tightly, and with big, bright, open smiles. Meanwhile when I was seven years old a photographer at Sears said to my mother, "I bet I can make her smile!" and she was like, "Good luck!" and that's why I still have a closed-lipped portrait of me as a kid with my arms crossed and a very active bitch face.

I loved that Jon loved his family. But I wanted him to love me more than anyone. That's what I thought marriage was, loving another person more than anyone. What could possibly be the point otherwise?

The first time I went home with him for Christmas, before we were engaged, we all sat around the same dinner table eating the same meal and having the same conversation. I remember thinking, *I don't know how to do this.* As I opened presents in front of people I didn't really know yet and struggled with how I should act I thought, *I don't know how to do this*. But when we were shuttled into separate bedrooms, and he snuck into my room anyway so we could have sex under his parents' roof, breaking the rules, I thought, *now this I know how to do*.

Some Questions for Men in Engagement Photos

This . . . wasn't your idea was it?

When you were younger could you ever have imagined yourself striking these poses unironically? With that expression on your face? While wearing that outfit?

But a cardigan? But you're in a rowboat? Are you trying to tell me that's your preferred rowing cardigan?

Why are you strolling through a desert? But people die out there?

Or leaning against the doorway of what looks to be an abandoned warehouse? It seems like maybe it was abandoned for a good reason? Are you in the Mob? An extra on *Law & Order*? Lost?

Why are you at the zoo? Who goes to the zoo on purpose other than children and tourists?

Why are you balancing on rocks? Did you create this rock scenario together or were you location scouting with your photographer when you came upon the rocks and you looked at one another as if to say, "Rocks. *Of course.*"

Why are you picking apples together near an antique John Deere tractor? Actually that one kind of makes sense.

Why are you in a marsh? On a footbridge? Sitting in a lifeguard chair? Naked in a tub together? In a snowstorm holding a hand-lettered sign featuring a pun about your future joint last name? Swinging on swings together or on a carousel or eating cotton candy? Again, are you children? Must you make that heart shape with your hands? Wait, are those deer behind you? Didn't you know they're like public transportation for ticks?

Circling back to the hand-lettered sign. Does it contain some sort of folksy and/or gendered wisdom about marriage? Who was the philosopher, HomeGoods? Sorry but there is just no way in hell that thing was your idea.

Hold on just a minute. Why are you juggling? Do you *know* how to juggle? Are you fake juggling? Do I need to insert a monocle emoji here?

Why are you wading into the ocean fully clothed?

Or standing dead center on a covered bridge? You know cars still drive on that, right?

Why are you standing out in the middle of a field? You know that doesn't mean your marriage will be outstanding in its field, right? Engagements are not dad jokes, sir. And sorry, I can't belabor this enough, there are *so many* ticks.

Why are you on the edge of a cliff? Yes, it's certainly stunning but did you know since 2011, 256 people have died taking precarious selfies and while I know this isn't technically a selfie it *is* an opportunity for me to ask you this question—why won't you demonstrate some fucking common sense for a change?

Also: Why a tie? But you're on a cliff? Is it a formal cliff? A business cliff? A you-never-get-a-second-chance-to-make-a-first-impression cliff?

Also not for nothing, did you know when you hold your fiancée up like that, with her legs wrapped around your waist, both strangers and her parents alike now know what you guys look like when you do it in that position?

No?

Well.

Back to the whole cardigan thing, do you wear them in real life? Never mind! I don't want to know!

Have you ever smiled with your mouth and all your teeth so close to another person's mouth and exposed teeth? It's weird, no? Is that your natural smile? Are you *sure*? Or is that what a dog person might call a "submissive smile"?

Do you realize how little you know right now?

Do you appreciate how happy you'll be, long after today, to have evidence that at one point in your life picking two silly outfits you both agreed on was considered "clearing a major hurdle"? It wasn't like you were trying to get an IEP for your kid or putting your dog down, your parents weren't dying and you weren't worried about what you'd do now that you'd lost your job. It wasn't looking at one another and wondering if you still loved each other at all, wondering what it felt like to have your photos taken at this, the beginning. Never seeing an end. You just looked at each other and agreed, "Yes that tie looks nice with those pants and complements your dress." *Whew.*

Do you have any idea how young you are? My god, you are so young. And so full of hope. And maybe a little dumb? But that's okay. We all were.

Could you rethink the legs around the waist thing, though?

Philosophical Frogs

October 1, 1997

Kimberly, my love,

A lot has happened since I began this letter. My mom is now gone, no more suffering, no more pain. It's been hard and I am so blessed to have you to help me through this tough time. Your love, your comfort, your shoulder, your hugs, your reassurance and support. I love you so much. I want you here right now.

I remember hearing about you, the girl who bleached her hair and I remember meeting you at Rialto and immediately falling for your sense of humor, your wit, and of course your beauty. You had me then. Then asking you out on a date (which took a lot of nerve) and the ensuing date, I knew you were the one. You accepted me as I was. You saw me with long hair, drunk and stupid, just a plain idiot, and you still saw something in me.

I know we never thought we would even marry anyone, but after being with you, I knew I would marry you. You demonstrated a kind of love that was amazing. You knew I would be the one for you. I remember giving you flowers and your reaction, I remember you telling me about your past and me telling you about mine. I remember thinking I was not worthy of you. You changed my life. I thought you were the best thing that ever happened to me and I still feel that way. You are my best friend, we share everything. You keep me sane, I feel lost without you. You are there when I need you, always compassionate, always loving. You accept me and my faults, you are nurturing, never condescending. You mean everything to me. I appreciate everything you do for me.

I've always had a really hard time expressing my feelings the way I want to. One of my many flaws. And there you are, standing by me through thick and thin, you are always there for me. I am so, so appreciative of the things you've done, the sacrifices you've made. I can't think of anyone I'd rather spend the rest of my life with.

You mean everything to me.

I love you.

Jon
Your husband
Your friend
Your love

October 6, 1997

My journal

"*Why the hell is there a disco ball hanging from the ceiling?*" I hissed between an incredibly fake smile, "*and what the hell are these lights doing here? I talked to you 2 days ago and said that I didn't want a lighting package!*"

The DJ sort of scratched his head and quickly went, "*Oh shit, that's right. Well, it's not going to kill you, is it?*"

It's not going to kill me, IS IT?

I brushed my veil over my shoulder, fixed my smile and replied, "No, I guess it won't," and proceeded directly to the bar, cut the line and demanded a glass of white wine. Fuck, I was paying for it after all. The main advantage of being the bride: no one wants to piss you off no matter how much of a bitch you're being. Not to mention the fact that you can cut in line anywhere—in the bathroom, at the bar, at the buffet.

One could reasonably say Jon and I began our marriage on different footing. He had been plummeted into grief over the death of his mother, Janie, just four days before our wedding. She had endured an intense seven-year struggle with ovarian cancer, one that had permeated his entire adult life. And yet he was expected to perform happiness, the happiest he had ever been, actually, because he had just gotten married. But me? I was on top of the world, celebrating the beginning of my Real Life—*finally*—while pausing occasionally to record my petty grievances. It's taken me twenty-three years to realize that if I could go back and redo just one week of our marriage it would be this one. The very first one.

Our wedding was everything a wedding tends to be— perfect and chaotic, gorgeous and melancholy. I had found my dress before I was even engaged (do you sense a theme?). I had flown to LA for a weekend of wedding dress shopping with my best friend from college and actual engaged person, Rachel. We browsed through a Jewish thrift store on our first morning in the city and I laid my hands on a stunning vintage Elizabeth Arden gown in pristine shape, jammed into one of the racks like it was just any other thing. This was when drop-dead gorgeous vintage, especially formal vintage, was still readily available and cheap. The golden age. That gown looked and fit as if it had been both designed and placed there only for me. It was ten dollars.

I filled two big black sketchbooks with an intersection of vintage inspiration, '90s Pacific Northwest looks, and the heyday of *Martha Stewart Weddings*. I taped in images of monochromatic hydrangea-heavy bouquets, Chanel Lucite platforms worthy of a modern (and wealthier) Cinderella, 1940s finger waves, vamp-colored nails and lips. I shut my mother out of the planning, sending her a letter stating that she wasn't allowed to swoop in and take a victory lap. I felt that I had made this good life myself. I was left to research best practices and etiquette on my own then taped those printouts into my sketchbooks, too.

Jon and I were married at Oaks Pioneer Church, a tiny historic wedding chapel surrounded by rose bushes and looming pines. As the judge began the ceremony he asked for a moment of silence for Janie and a few quiet sobs jumped up to fill the space.

That day and into the evening I smiled more than I had probably ever smiled in my life, which I hope means something to every man I've crossed paths with from the time I was a child who told me how much prettier I would look if I just smiled more. My face actually hurt.

We cried over the toast from Jon's dad, delivered by Jon's uncle in his absence, written as he grieved in the home where he had just lost his own wife. I cried when my grandparents got out on the dance floor, because it was them I thought of as we planned the reception at Monte Carlo, with its deep red velvet flocked wallpaper and serving trays of pasta. Everyone loaded their plates with what they thought was maybe potatoes but turned out to be bread pudding and no one cared. This was a party. A sad, beautiful, rowdy party.

One of the most iconic portraits our photographer shot that night was not of us, but was instead of one of my friends from LA wearing a vintage red smoking jacket that nearly matched the wallpaper. He is looking directly into the camera, a single eyebrow raised, a lit cigarette dangling from the slight smile on his lips, as he is about to place his lighter back in his pocket. It felt like a night when everyone was young and would be forever. No habit too dangerous, no outfit too outrageous, no regrets too insurmountable.

We had budgeted carefully for our wedding if you consider "budgeting carefully" a phrase that still applies when you have no savings and are reliant on vague promises from other people. My father had told us he would help with the costs, so I sent him regular budget breakdowns that he never responded to. He had helped me frequently in the past, too frequently according to letters from my stepmother sent without his knowledge, so there was no reason to doubt his offer.

When we got back to our hotel room on our wedding night, drunk and spent and over the moon, I pushed through the pile of cards to find his. In it, there was a check for a few hundred dollars. I was drunk and stunned and realized how freshly fucked we were. I cried and then I changed into a different dress and we went to another hotel room where all our friends were still partying and we never even had sex that night.

I didn't even dance with my father at my wedding, a fact that only registered days later when he brought it up in casual conversation with a catch in his voice. Jon and I had decided against having traditional mother-son, father-daughter, or any combination of parent-child dances given the absence of his parents. But still, this was not an insurmountable challenge. My grandfather managed to dance with me as did my stepfather. This was not hard. You ask the bride to dance, especially when she is your daughter.

If hell is other people, trying to clearly communicate with them cannot be far behind.

When Jon left for Alaska to be with his family the week before our wedding I didn't know if we'd be going on a honeymoon. No one could begrudge a man who just lost his mother for not wanting to spend five weeks driving around the country. I couldn't imagine trying to drag him north to south, west to east, coast-to-coast, on some sort of forced tour of happiness. I left the decision up to him, expecting we would postpone. But when he arrived back in Portland just three days before the wedding and two days after his mom died, grief as fresh as it could possibly be, he said, "I want to go. I want to get away from all of this" and I was thrilled. Who was I to question it aside from someone who didn't want to question it at all?

We promised only our grandparents we'd stop and stay with them along the way, otherwise we planned each day as it came, and who could possibly argue with that? Eight days after our wedding, on my twenty-ninth birthday, we were at Big Mantrap Lake in Minnesota, visiting Jon's maternal grandmother. She had just lost one of her daughters and I remember her not wanting to talk about it. I think she said it was "too bad" and we dropped it. Her daughter, Jon's mother, had died and yet somehow "dropping it" seemed like the right decision. *Yes of course,* I thought.

His grandmother had her own year-round house on the lake, but we stayed down the road in the big family cabin, The Pines.

Every night, crisp and cool, Jon built a fire in the fireplace and we'd stretch out in front of it, surrounded by his family history. We pulled out photo albums, autograph books, and scrapbooks stuffed with mementos and letters. Most of the items had belonged to his great-grandparents, William and Mabel, who had built the cabin. We read the best ones aloud to one another.

Postmarked SEP 18 1906 230PM

Mable Dear,

Not able to come up Sunday evening to the greatest of my sorrow and delight of your pleasure. I will try and write you a few of the following unexpressable words that it would be impossible for me to tell in a personal conversation. When I frist beheld your angelic perfections I was bewildered and my brain whirled around like a bumblebee in a glass tumbler. My eyes stood open like a cellar door in a country town as I lifted my ears to catch the silvery accents of your sweet voice my tongue refused to wag, and in silent adoration I drank in the sweet infections of love as a thirsty man swallows a tumbler of hot whisky punch. Since the light of your face fell upon my life I some times feel as if I could lift myself up by my suspenders to the top of the church steeples and pull the bell rope for Sunday evening church. May these kind words of love and happiness rest forever in the mind of my loving little Mable, and in the coming years when the shadows grow from yonder hills and the evening sun sets in its glorious beauty, the philosophical frogs sings his cheerfull evening hyms, the beautyfull clear notes shrill through my

brains, your happy in anothers love, can come and shed a
tear and catch a cold upon the last resting place of Yours
Truly Wm.
     Written with a smile. Will behave the next time. End.
Think of me when you are lonely.

Those five weeks laid bare how narrow our lives were in Portland. The one house, the two jobs, the same restaurants, the
small circumference of experiences, the liberal politics. But this
country is a big place, a big mess of a place, full of boredom,
beauty, and bullshit.

We had silverware tossed across a table at us by a waitress in
Butte, Montana, and saw a sign at another café that read "We'll
put bacon on anything! Just ask!" We hit the McRock N' Roll
Cafe in Bismarck, North Dakota, which is what happens when a
regular McDonald's tries to be a Hard Rock Cafe. I ate my fries
to the right of Kim Basinger's 1971 yearbook photo, and let the
record show Kim Basinger is neither rock nor roll. We went to a
Fleetwood Mac show at the Fargodome because we heard an
ad for it on the radio when we were within sixty miles of the
city. We snagged what felt like the absolute last hotel room on
Earth, peppered with cigarette burn holes and with the dreary
ambiance of a crime scene. Soft-core porn was available on the
TV so we watched some.

We mostly ate in diners and at truck stops. At Ray's Southside
Restaurant in Baldwin, Wisconsin, a customer asked a waitress
how it was going and as she poured a cup of coffee she shouted
across, "Oh you know, boring as ever." We ate Chicago-style
stuffed pizza in actual Chicago and Jon pushed back from the
table to announce, "I just had my ass kicked by a pizza." In Ohio
we met up with one of my best friends from high school who

retold one of my favorite stories, the one about her brilliant older brother finding her diary and correcting it for punctuation—humiliating, devastating, objectively hilarious. He went on to be a double doctor, MD and PhD, naturally. On our way to Rochester, New York, we discovered Niagara Falls was only twenty miles away so we detoured. We bought those ballpoint pens with the water inside and a little man in a barrel going over the falls, depending on how you tipped it.

We camped at Chittenden Brook Campground in Vermont, never venturing too far from the fire, and curled into tight balls at night to stay warm. We ate breakfast at a café just outside Bethel and it was the first true maple syrup of our trip. When we set out on our honeymoon I told Jon we should use our trip to think about where else we might want to live. I already knew life had a way of running away with you and suddenly a city you thought you'd live in for a year or two becomes six years or eight and you end up hating it but by then you're stuck.

We drove through Virginia as both of us were coming down with colds and that entire stretch felt mildly hallucinatory. An eighteen-wheeler was bearing down on us, a giant cross of amber lights studded onto its grill. I felt a bit panicked, like Jesus himself was chasing us.

When we got to Delray Beach my grandparents threw us a party and when I stood with all the ladies for a photo one of them shouted to another, "Remember when we were that tall?!" We went on a day cruise to the Bahamas, started drinking beer on the ship at 10:30 a.m., and once we docked I spent an hour and a half getting cornrows, which was obviously a mistake.

We ended up in a bar called the Salty Dog in the Florida panhandle after driving and driving unsuccessfully trying to find another cool little beach town after blazing too hastily past

Apalachicola. When we told our waitress how far we had driven that day she replied, "That's enough to just piss you off, ain't it?"

We got a hotel upgrade in the French Quarter because we were on our honeymoon; the French doors of our fancy second floor room opened right out onto Bourbon Street. We went to a strip club, Maiden Voyage, and I said to Jon, "Let's get you a table dance. Which girl do you want?" The next night in Austin, Halloween night, we navigated streets packed with costumed strangers, including a rib-eye steak being chased by a fork and steak knife. We discovered La Fiesta in Pecos, Texas, and I thought Jon was having an honest-to-goodness heart attack so much so that I started to rise from my seat—to do what exactly I'm not sure. It took me a beat to realize it was the heat from their house salsa that he was experiencing, not a cardiac event.

We drove through Roswell and Santa Fe and Dixon, finally stopping overnight in Taos to recover, do laundry, and eat more. Rabbits with death wishes were determined to get under our car tires as we drove out before the sun rose, with the silhouette of the Sangre de Cristo mountain range behind us.

After driving for nine hours we discovered the hard way that it was too late in the season to visit the North Rim of the Grand Canyon. But since we were already there, we decided to drive yet another four and a half hours to get to the South Rim. We assumed we'd crash at the Bright Angel Lodge, not realizing those were the kind of arrangements you needed to make months if not years in advance. Ultimately, we paid twenty bucks to park, took a few photos of my grouchy face, bought some postcards, and left. And that was the Grand Canyon.

We stayed overnight in a cabin in the Kaibab National Forest, wound our way through red rock, along rivers, and ranchland and across southern Utah. We hustled through Idaho, stopped in

Pendleton, Oregon, at a motel for the last night of our trip, and then moments later threw everything back in our car. There had been dead flies in the bathroom sink and the bathtub, sure, but a spider crawling out from under the covers when I whipped them back to take a better look at the brown and red stains on the bedspread was . . . the absolute last straw.

We dragged ourselves back into Portland on November 7—five weeks after we had left, five weeks after our wedding, almost six weeks after Jon's mother had died—arriving at 2:30 in the morning. The car hadn't broken down once, we didn't even get a flat tire. We didn't get a single speeding ticket or parking ticket. We didn't get into any accidents, thank God, since that's pretty much all I thought about the entire time, absentmindedly stomping my foot on a phantom brake pedal on the passenger side when Jon drove. We had perfect weather just about everywhere we went.

We had traveled all these roads and highways, seen sunrise after sunset, listened to Stevie Nicks sing "Landslide" in person. *Oh, mirror in the sky, what is love? Can the child within my heart rise above?* But a honeymoon can't fix grief. Nothing can "fix" it, really. I think I might've assumed moving forward meant moving on. That all we had to do was put all those miles between us and loss. I didn't know yet that grief, especially that depth of grief, wasn't something you just moved on or away from. Especially when it is mostly silent, mostly hidden. Especially when I assumed Jon was coping because he never overtly said, "Look at me. Can you see me? I am grieving." Because I somehow believed if I just didn't bring it up he wouldn't remember. I didn't want to remind him, as if he had somehow forgotten.

I wish I had said to him that week, *maybe, let's not go.* I wish I had said to him that week, *I think you need to talk to someone, if not now then soon. And certainly if not me, then absolutely someone, please.* I wish I had said, *I don't know what to do but I promise not to ignore this.* But I ignored it. Because I didn't understand it and ignoring it was easier.

Ignoring it would always be easier.

Why Did You Get Married?

Did you marry for love?

Is that what it was?

Were you genuinely, completely, madly in love? Did you fall into a relationship, progress neatly toward engagement, have the wedding of your dreams? Did the minor glitches here and there not matter because what could possibly be more important than your love? Did you think people who got cold feet should've listened and you couldn't imagine feeling anything but absolute certainty when you said *yes*? Did you think you knew everything?

Or was your relationship raw and physical and, honey, that was plenty? Those eyes, that hair, this arm, that leg, the necklace that fell just so over a collarbone, that watch on that wrist, that smile inside that mouth, were a package of parts that, well, helloooo? You were evaluating each other like racehorses, enamored with shiny coats and sure legs, but did you understand this phase was on a timer?

Did you want that ol' chestnut, security? To know you promised in a church or a courthouse and in front of everyone who mattered that for the rest of your life you would pay your bills on time? Did you find yourself sizing up potential partners as a good mother? A plausible father? Trustworthy and stable? Someone who could be relied on to make balanced meals, 401(k) contributions, and carpool commitments? Is this what it was going to come down to? And who could blame you? No one goes into this thinking choosing a violent fuckup is a super idea.

Or did you have a baby first, doing everything all out of order, then cave to the pressure to "make it official"? Did you think marriage paled in comparison to making a person together so what's the big deal? Did you find out you were wrong? Or were you right? Or were you worried you had already invested too much time? Were you too exhausted to think of starting all over again with someone new? Did you not realize one year or three, five or even ten would feel so small compared to the long slow glow of your life to come? What would you have lost? What would you have gained?

Or did you just want to climb that ladder of success, Mr. Big Shot? Fine, you said it. To another tax bracket, another social bracket, a world where ladders and brackets mattered? Did you want The Name? Was it everything you ever wanted and, yes, turns out most of the things you wanted in life *were* things?

Did you wonder when your life would start? Did you find yourself attending weddings at a relentless rate and thinking, *When will that be me, that will never be me, when will it be me?* Did you start to believe that without this ring, this save the date, this color palette, this florist, this dress, this shower and this other shower and this bachelorette party, this ceremony, this first dance, that toast and this other toast, these photographs, and this honeymoon, no one would know you were successfully working through The Checklist?

Or did you save someone? Did you give them a reason to stop using, stop drinking, stop all their absolute bullshit? Did you leap from the frying pan right into the motherfucking fire? Or was your partner just as broken as you were and together you made one whole, healthy person? Does it scare you to think of your relationship in those terms? Because whenever anything goes wrong—and something will go wrong, this being life—suddenly you will feel less than? You defined yourself as half of something and where did that get you?

Did you finally just give in? Did you know from the start it wasn't what you wanted but you couldn't come up with a good enough reason to say no? Was this a good person so what was the problem? Had you already sent the invitations? Put down deposits? Could you imagine anything more humiliating than a canceled wedding? Did you weigh the potential disappointment of others as more important than your own? Did you realize that's what you were doing? Or did you just think it was nerves, you silly goose? Did you do it to make your parents proud? Is this what they wanted most of all? Did he check all the boxes? Was she the daughter they never had? What else could you possibly do?

Did you ever wonder why it mattered so much? Did you ever attempt to trace how weddings and marriage got into your head in the first place? Life and books and movies had been training you from the start. They told you men were hot and charming but also the enemy and relationships were wars to be relentlessly fought. Wait two days to call—no, three. Ask him about himself, men love to talk about themselves. Flatter, flatter, flatter. Listen. Be the best listener! There were strategies and five-point plans. There was lingerie to wear and looks to practice in the mirror. But what if you suddenly found, with a member of the enemy camp, it was possible and preferable to simply be on the same side?

Were you framed as a future bride and a future mommy when you were just a little girl? I was having breakfast with a friend last summer and there was a baby being bounced and comforted in that restaurant. A grandmother at another table, no doubt feeling nostalgic, leaned over to her granddaughter and said, "The next time there's a baby in our family, it'll probably be yours!" Her granddaughter looked at her and replied evenly, "I'm eleven."

Or did you feel like you were shut out of the conventional

marriage conversation completely because of your sexuality, your physicality, your fluidity, your disability? Because of where you lived or who you were? Did you tell yourself you didn't care anyway, it was so basic and what idiot would want *that*? But, as it turned out, that basic idiot was you? Was it the cultural validation it implied? Or was it just practical? The right to visit in the hospital, to inherit the house, to not have to explain your relationship to every goddamn person for a goddamn change? The ease of holding up a hand with a ring on it that implied *I am loved, I have committed, I am legit, I am just like you, you are not better than me*?

Did you want to be seen as good and worthy? As a normal person who could do normal things for a fucking change? Were you energized by the power of those rings and that day, it all somehow bestowing upon you immediate moral superiority? Even though you were the same flawed, fucked-up person you were just 24 hours before?

Did you keep your vows? Did you cherish? Were you there in sickness and not a total bitch about it? Did you avoid all the forms of infidelity—not just the fucking, which is obvious and cliché—but the flirty texting, the wishing for someone else, the emotional investments you made hoping for a return? What if monogamy was stupid? What if it wasn't?

Was love all you needed all along? Was that what the members of your wedding party said in their toasts? That as long as you had love, and you clearly had so much of that, you were pretty much set? No work to be done, nothing to change, just love forever and ever, amen.

Why did you get married?

Was it love?

Of course it was.

I married for love, too.

What else could it be?

Life Is Better on Weed

This is how it will feel when you have everything.

It will not be without stress or worry. But the stress and the worry will feel pure, like it's the good, honest work of life. It will feel manageable, something that lives within the confines of a normal business day, bank hours. And it will be a relief because the stress and worry will bring results for a change. It won't just be free-floating fear of death or middle-of-the-night staring contests with the ceiling. It won't be the persistent thrum of stress and worry from the previous few years. That stress and worry only dragged me down and then down again.

Jon and I moved across the country, from Oregon to Vermont, for my new full-time job. I had gone from freelance to a design studio job to a partnership in another design studio that teetered on the brink of ruin in the wake of 9/11. This new job paid me at regular intervals and I no longer had to worry about bringing work in the door. I laid that burden down and felt light again. Hopeful. The amount of my check would always be the same, I would have health insurance. I couldn't get over how thrilling this was, this type of old-fashioned yet surprisingly sexy stability I took for granted at my very first job out of college. Back when the world worked just so. I couldn't believe I would be able to see a dentist again without having to pay in cash. I even had a 401(k). *Meow.*

Jon and I left behind a miscarriage at twelve weeks. There was no heartbeat found on the same day we had organized a group lunch to tell my business partners and some of our friends our big news. The irony was I had wasted most of my all-too-brief pregnancy bracing for loss then was completely unprepared when it came. I thought knowing the statistic, that 1-in-4 statistic, would arm me. But it didn't. I didn't know, didn't want to know, that even after having heard a heartbeat at eight weeks, the odds of miscarrying were still there. I didn't know, didn't want to know, that although those odds were only 3 percent, that would be exactly where I'd fall, and I'd keep right on falling.

I felt broken and sad beyond belief. It stung and shocked like a slap across the face. It wouldn't have mattered if, before that slap, someone had gently patted my face and said, "One day it'll feel like this but so much harder." On top of that, I hadn't told anyone, I hadn't allowed myself to feel the joy I should have. I had experienced pre-misery that didn't alleviate the real misery, not one bit.

I thought watching a sad movie in my head would prepare me for any real sadness that might come. But nothing can prepare you for not hearing a heartbeat when your heart is preparing for everything except that. Nothing can prepare you for stillness when just a few weeks before you had seen that fast little electric pulse, a flickering firefly, and that space inside you was undulating with possibility. Nothing can prepare you for death when you were expecting life. It wasn't a baby yet, but a future. It was small T-shirts and a name, Sawyer. It was a car seat in the backseat that I could already imagine, I would pretend to glance in the rearview mirror and smile at a baby that was not there yet. We were going to be more than a couple—we were going to be a family. We would have it all. And then all of that was gone.

We left behind his friends, my friends, our friends. We left behind a city that felt like home. Portland was where we wanted to have babies and raise them alongside people we loved in a place we understood. But having all the plans in the world doesn't mean much. It didn't mean we got to stay. It didn't mean we were allowed to have the baby I got pregnant with. It didn't mean we were allowed to follow a path we thought we had seen so clearly.

It meant that somehow I was going through my third recession and had gotten no better at preparing for one. It meant our own deficit spending had left us on the verge of financial collapse. And it meant, against all odds, I had still somehow managed to secure a job on the other side of the country that paid me twice what I had been making. It meant the life we had loved in a place we had loved had turned so dark and hopeless we were being forced out of it. We felt like we had no choice but to burn it all down.

We drove away, like cowards, the flames in our rearview mirror.

We rented an old farmhouse in a town with a population of ten thousand in northern Vermont. That farmhouse was on Weed Road. I hadn't smoked pot since 1993 and had no intention of ever doing so again but that didn't keep me from making a truly relentless barrage of "Life is better on Weed" jokes. Because it was.

I had found the house during an intense four-day window, after driving one of our cars cross-country by myself. My tasks were to deposit the car at a friend's house, secure a place for us to live, and fly back. And I had done all those things. I had the fresh energy that comes when things start going your way again. Every chore a thrill, every concrete task welcomed with open arms.

I had sifted through the thin classified section of the thin local paper. I didn't know then that that paper would diminish even more over time, eventually representing a collection of *USA Today* and AP stories with a front-page photo of something local, followed by a pile of ads and inserts. But that's where I had found it, a farmhouse for rent on a country road for $1,500 a month. My friend Joe went with me to take a look and neither of us could quite believe it. We tried to seem cool when mostly what we were doing was racing from room to room, him passing me and mouthing, "Are you fucking kidding me?" The pressed tin ceiling, the wrought iron hinges. Wide plank floors. A looming red barn across that lone road. A fireplace in the kitchen, cobbled together from fat stones. Massive bookshelves built into massive rooms.

It was falling down, to be sure. The windows were old and thin and barely still held in place by their sashes. They rattled with the wind, like the old rattling teeth they were. This house, Jon and I often joked, was on its slow return to the earth. We didn't know yet the return would be faster than we imagined. But it was everything I had in my mind when we told people we were moving to Vermont.

It was the postcard.

I was overwhelmed by it.

It was the feeling of having survived, it was the feeling of being rewarded for suffering. It was that feeling of our shitty fortunes beginning to reverse themselves. I wanted to fall to my knees in gratitude. I thought we would never climb out of the stress and despair, now look at us. We had historically done best when our enemy was a common one. Lost jobs, lost babies, illness, death, failure. All the hits.

For the first time since I was a teenager living in my mother's house, I could look outside in the morning and see a rural landscape—forest, field, the wide-open sky, wildflowers. One day those fields would be carved up and sold off, but we would be long gone by then. I would later drive by and glare at the oversize houses occupying the land, identical cedar play structures dotting each yard. A farm for raising families.

I remember when that field grew wild and felt like a sponge underfoot. I trudged through it in rain boots; I knew the exact spots where the water was likely to seep up under the pressure of my step. Seventeen years later I can feel it still, the softness, the sucking thunk when I pulled my foot from the mud—sometimes I'd accidentally pull my foot right out of my boot, left stuck in the muck. In the winter, with the field full of snowdrifts, it felt like trying to walk through the ocean. The wind would whip across and leave tears streaking across my cheeks and what did it matter? I was alive. The sky was here only for me and Jon. We deserved that sky. Even in the thickest of blizzards I could look back toward the house and see the lights on, knowing my husband was inside, the heat hissing and popping, and I would tell myself, "This is real. Look at us."

We had an obnoxious amount of space in that house and we wanted to fill it with everything from every thrift store we entered, where it felt like everything cost a quarter. It's impossible to recall now what completely empty weekend days felt like. We would sleep in, walk the dogs, hop in the car, grab a coffee at the local coffee shop, and just drive. I grew up roaming the spider web of country roads in my hometown for hours and this part felt like home. We found thrift stores ten minutes, twenty minutes, more than an hour away, and we went to all of them. We hauled back 1970s ski hats, 1960s ski sweaters, 1980s snowmobile suits. Sometimes we hung out at bars after a thrift store hit and drank ourselves drunk, talking to complete strangers. Then we would get ourselves home, back out to the country, and wake to another day looking out over those fields.

Sure, the foundation was fieldstone and when there was a rainstorm we could hear the water rush through our house, literally under our feet. And yes, there was a snake in our kitchen once, Jon gingerly carrying it out to the yard using a pair of kitchen tongs. Crickets called to each other from different rooms, "Hello, can you hear me?" "I can hear you, can you hear me?" We wanted space and we got space. We wanted wild and we got wild. We had everything we wanted and most things we had never dreamed of.

On one of the first warm spring days, so welcome and energizing, we decided to dig through the abandoned corn crib next to the farmhouse. It was exquisitely weathered, sitting atop a rock foundation, and full of the abandoned belongings of people who had lived in the farmhouse long before us. We found old pale blue and green bottles and piles of screen prints. A stack of old skis, a cow's skull, yearbooks, rusted tin cans, and a rocking chair I dragged inside and would end up nursing our first baby in. I still have it. Jon found a single pair of white roller skates that unbelievably fit me perfectly. I still have those, too.

We had moved from a 600 square foot house in Oregon into a 2,500 square foot farmhouse in Vermont, selling and giving away everything we could before we left Portland. We hadn't remotely filled all that new space yet, although we were certainly giving it our best shot. So what choice did I have but to lace up those roller skates and skate around our empty living room after work like it was a thing people did? My body instinctively recalled how to cross over on the corners.

That first summer we would sit outside after work, have a beer, and feel the heavy summer air settle all around us. More than once the pregnant whoosh of a burner would startle us and I'd turn to see a hot air balloon gliding up, up, up over our house, the fields, so close. I would look up, my chin pointing to the sky, my mouth naturally dropped open. If there is a better feeling than your life working out while you are fully aware it is working out, I'm not sure what that might be, how it could feel any more visceral and full of wonder than this.

Then the sun would set and bats would pour out of our attic. It's strange we weren't just a bit more horrified by that. We would watch them exit at dusk, swoop and swerve, screech and chirp, and thank them for vacuuming up mosquitoes. Some nights we would count them, barely able to see our beers in front of our faces, and watch their silhouettes. 1, 5, 15, 22, 37, 52! We'd light one cigarette off another and ignite our conversations about work and Vermont and the house and our new lives with even more alcohol, the bats still swooping and clicking.

Sometimes we would take our dogs down to the river near our farmhouse and go swimming. I look back now and realize there was probably all kinds of shit in that river, literal and chemical. Odds are we were downstream from at least one farm. It's a miracle we didn't swallow *E. coli*. Even when we were in the water we knew there were rusted barrels nearby but we still had an absurd belief everything in the country was clean and right when I knew from personal experience it's often just a beautiful setting for burying things.

I wonder now if perhaps the happiest you can ever be is when you don't know too much, when you don't know what's happening right under your feet, when you trust everything is just as it appears.

After this Rumspringa of relief, the transition of the move, and the time spent settling in, I was ready. I was worried we were losing too much time when it came to getting pregnant again, even though we had desperately needed that time to recover. As it turned out, I got pregnant often in that farmhouse. Those pregnancies were not accidents but instead the result of a carefully monitored breeding program that could only be brought to you by ovulation kits and information. Peeing on a stick in the bathroom at work felt like thrilling practice for taking a pregnancy test. I lived in a parallel universe every day when I showed up to work, an ovulation kit burning a hole in my bag. My coworkers, of course, had no idea I'd be sticking my fingers in my vagina to check my cervical mucus then peeing on a stick in the bathroom, potentially followed by a whole lot of fucking once I got home.

This wasn't how we (or anyone) planned to make a baby but this is where I had pushed us. I was terrified that by choosing to put off getting pregnant right after we were married, as family and strangers alike would prefer, we had been cavalier. Then our unplanned pregnancy followed by an even more unplanned miscarriage had been our punishment. As if the universe cared at all whether another human baby was born or when. Jon had faith it would work out—he always had faith things would work out, regardless of the category or degree of challenge—but he also knew going along would ease my irrational (according to men) and relatable (according to women) fertility panic.

A friend who had gotten pregnant accidentally told me to stop messing around with regular pregnancy tests and buy the digital ones. She had taken enough pregnancy tests in a panic to know. On one of my long drives home from work, I finally stopped at a drugstore and bought those pregnancy tests and a big bag of York Peppermint Patties from the Halloween candy aisle.

The next morning when I looked down at the stick and saw

PREGNANT I couldn't have known yet I would go on to assign mythical powers to that test, that specific drugstore, and that candy for the rest of my life. It was the combination that did it. Don't talk to me about biology and facts.

Every time I had a positive pregnancy test when we lived in that farmhouse—in three years I would have three of them—I'd take our dogs for a walk down the dirt road to the left of the field I loved. There was only one other house on that road and since it was a short dirt road that connected two more substantial roads I felt safe walking it alone. Well, walking it alone with two dogs, which is different.

I had decided going forward that I wouldn't shrink from feeling happy for as long as that happiness might last. Of course I had a new full-time job and no real friends yet, so it wasn't like I was going to go around and shout my pregnancy news from the rooftops, either. But I allowed myself to go into it clear-eyed. To force my disaster-prone brain to just absorb the damn joy for a change. And even if the worst happened, I accepted that all the pessimism in the world wouldn't have made a difference either way.

I'd whisper to myself as I walked our dogs and they sniffed around, nosing past Queen Anne's lace and peeing on bachelor's button. I would say to this baby who was not yet a baby, "I am happy you are here. I love you already. I want you to stay, I hope you will stay, but if you can't, if something is wrong, if you can't hang on, it's okay to let go."

Twice these babies-in-waiting would stay. One, a phantom, would let go. And I was convinced this walk had something to do with it, that it was a matter of free will for a bunch of cells. I liked that version then and I still like it now. I am still convinced it was the drugstore and the test, Peppermint Patties and the walk down a dirt road with two dogs. These were the winning numbers on the combination lock of my life.

They unlocked everything.

When I had a baby, I didn't understand I had unwittingly kicked open the door to an entirely different life. I didn't understand it because it doesn't happen immediately. I thought it was just the sleep thing, the tiredness thing, the baby crying and pooping, the breast milk. All that living in my body as an actual body, a bone hanger draped in blood and flesh, muscle and milk. I was so used to thinking of my body as the thing that held up my head and I put clothes on and I was perpetually disappointed in. I thought it was just the thing I had sex with but, good grief, turns out the body is an animal thing. Basic in its function, knowing better than I did as I nursed that my uterus would cramp, trying to shrink itself down to a more reasonable size. I would hear my son cry and my breasts would throb. Pardon me but, honestly, what the hell? I would feel both thrilled and more than a little insulted by how my body was just marching on, how my body didn't seem to need *me* at all.

This is how it felt when I had everything.

It felt animal and true.

I couldn't believe how much of everything I had.

I looked around at my life and it would look different through someone else's lens, I knew. The disintegrating house, the bats pouring out from under our roof. The porcupine that chewed on our house that one time. I could hear a rhythmic chonk-chonk-chonk and there he was, in broad daylight, eating the damn house.

There was that thunderstorm one afternoon when the sky cracked right open and released rivers from the sky. I hadn't showered in days because something was fucked up with the plumbing, so I walked outside and stood under the broken gutter.

I took my shirt off, angled my back to the road, and let the rain wash over me. It's weird, I thought, how much time we spend with our clothes on.

This is probably how nudists are born.

I think back now to the horses that often broke free from the neighbor's field; they would pop up in the deep, tall grass on the side of our house that contained an enormous picture window. There they would be, one white and one chestnut, standing with their swish-swish tails, and their twitchy-get-off-me ears, dipping down to pull grass with their teeth, as if they were sipping from a stream. That window was one of the first things that made my stomach flip when I came to take a look at that house. And now, with the horses there, and the bachelor's button and Queen Anne's lace blurring to dots of blue-purple and white among the electric green swaying outside, it was like I was watching an extremely slow-paced documentary about renegade horses, formatted correctly for my screen.

I remember the chug of the washing machine next to the kitchen, can still feel the cool cast iron of the enormous farmhouse sink, and see the liquid pink sunsets and the fire of the foliage in October at the top of the hill. I remember that one spot in the snow where a hawk had swooped down and liberated a mouse from its earthly home, the little tracks coming to a dead stop underneath an imprint of graduated wings. And what did that mouse think, as it was being lifted higher, higher, higher into the sky? Did it have a little mouse thought of how he should've appreciated it down there in his humble home, underneath the snow, with all his pals, or was he just too wowed by the view right before his death?

We learned keeper lessons in that house. Neither of us had been responsible for a house heated with oil before and we learned the hard way you best not let the oil get low. Because, guaranteed, on one of the coldest winter nights you could ever imagine, the last of the oil will get sucked from the tank, taking all the gunk and junk swirling around the bottom with it, and muck up the line. And it will seize up and shut down the whole shebang. I wouldn't find this out until bedtime, that, wait a minute, it's cold in here. Wait a minute, the heat isn't kicking on. Wait a minute, it's January and this is Vermont and my God we have an infant.

The three of us—I've forgotten what it was like for there to only be three of us—were sleeping in the living room already anyway. The single pane windows combined with old radiators made the bedroom unbearably cold. We weren't taking any chances with a baby going through his first winter. I dressed us both in layers and hats then buried us under as many blankets as I could find. I snuggled my son close and as afraid as I was of the cold, I relished I had one animal job—keep this baby warm. The purity of focus was both exhausting and a temporary, welcome release from all my other thoughts.

These were the years of basic needs and basic pleasures, patterns and epiphanies: A cold beer, a hot air balloon, a rushing river. A regular paycheck, a smoke at the end of the day, a found pair of roller skates that fit. Two dogs, three fields, one dirt road. The cycles of blinding white snow, Fruity Pebbles leaves, neon grass. Hawks airlifting mice, old green glass bottles foggy from age. A washing machine that chugs, a kitchen fireplace that smokes, a big glass rectangle that looks out on runaway horses. Begging life to stay with you, begging life to leave you before it can break your heart, the cramping uterus, the leaking breasts, the fear of freezing to death, fifty bats rushing out and swirling over your head. I was happy and I knew it. Clap your hands.

Help was here.

A man came out late in the night, trudging through the snow

to get to our front door. I heard him and Jon mumbling down in the basement, standing on that dirt floor. I heard clanging and wrenching, more muffled conversation. A laugh. A shout. Clang, clang. All the while I tried to keep the baby asleep.

The heat kicked back on.

We were saved. We were safe.

We, along with our two dogs, lived in that house for three years. When we moved out, to the first house we bought together, I was six months pregnant with our second child, a girl. I had taken that walk down that dirt road with our dogs. I had asked that baby to stay, but be free to go, and I would love them any which way.

She stayed.

Three years after we moved out, the farmhouse caught fire. Had I known it was coming, I would've stripped it of everything I had loved and could carry. No one had loved that rundown farmhouse like we had, at least not in a good long while. We would've taken the long hinges and ripped out the pressed tin ceiling. The wide plank floors, the stone fireplace, that picture window, the built-ins, that deep farmhouse sink. All turned to ash and char.

It's August now as I write this, almost seventeen years since we moved to Vermont. I was running an errand not far from where our old farmhouse once stood. I decided to drive by, as I often do when I'm out that way.

The last time I had stopped by was almost a year before, on a brilliant autumn day, a day so crisp and gorgeous it felt painful. I had driven down that short dirt road and pulled over. I thought about the times I had walked it with our dogs that have long since died. We scattered their ashes in a field just off that road, down near the riverbank where we used to swim. I thought about how I whispered, "I am happy you are here. I love you already. I want you to stay, I hope you will stay, but if you can't, if something is wrong, if you can't hang on, it's okay to let go." I thought about how I had spent my birthday afternoon all those years ago walking with a stroller on Weed Road, my baby boy just four months old, wearing a tiny little flannel button-down shirt and a blaze orange knit cap. The trees were glowing in golds, oranges, and reds just like they had back then. I sat in my car, put my head down on the steering wheel, and cried.

This time was different. It was the same time of year for the Queen Anne's lace and bachelor's button, that electric green grass. Every time I see them, no matter where I see them, I still think of the farmhouse and our first summer in Vermont, the mucky river and the horses. I think about how I had everything and I knew it.

I pulled over to take a photo of those wildflowers. I hadn't been stopped for more than two minutes when a pickup truck turned onto the same dirt road and pulled up right alongside me, my gut instinctively clenched. I looked up to see a young man with facial piercings, wearing a baseball cap, who asked politely, "Are you alright?" and I felt stunned by the question.

I thanked him.

Yes, I was alright.

I took a few photos then drove up the dirt road, stopping at that familiar stop sign, where it dead-ended onto Weed Road. I took the left I had taken hundreds of times before, past where our farmhouse and the corn crib used to stand. The land and lush summer vegetation had reclaimed it, completing its return. Not even the stone foundation left behind by the fire was visible. The lot had become a small field, overgrown with scrubby trees and tall grass.

It was like the house was never there.

It was like none of it had ever happened.

Now That We've Had a Baby My Terms and Conditions Have Changed

Thank you for choosing me ("Me") as the mother of your child. These terms ("Terms") govern your access to and use of my services ("Unpaid Labor"). Please read them carefully as I will bring up the most obscure aspects of this agreement during our next argument ("Discussion"). By using my services you agree to be bound by these Terms. Sort of like how by using your services I got pregnant and now look at us—updating Terms and Conditions already. Life comes at you fast.

1. PREVIOUS DESCRIPTION OF MY SERVICES

In our previous verbal agreement that took place in front of our family and friends but not in a church as your parents had hoped, I ("I") unwittingly agreed to perform a set of services ("Unpaid Labor") that, for the stability and longevity of our organization, must now be revisited. Statements like "to have and to hold" somehow came to encompass emotional support, financial support, spiritual support, laundry support, management of the household to a degree I had not fully appreciated, including regular selection and upgrading of linens, the selection and purchasing of all gifts for every occasion for every human being you have had any sort of meaningful contact with since we met, social calendar management, meal preparation management, pet management, vacation management, medical and dental appointment management, retirement funds management, and automobile management. In conclusion, all management-management. Also, blow jobs.

2. UPDATES TO OUR ORGANIZATION

As you are aware, our organization has grown exponentially with the addition of one infant ("Infant"). Your son ("Your Son") requires nourishment, primarily from my body, and around-the-clock care really anyone could provide. Just about anyone at all. This addition of 33.3% more human beings to our organization has understandably had a ripple effect. While some of the ripples are indeed on my body, they are also outside the purview of this agreement and by continuing to access my services you agree to shut up forever ("Forever") about those ripples. If you cannot keep your mouth shut about the ripples in my organization please skip to (9) ENDING THIS AGREEMENT.

3. UPDATED DIVISION OF SERVICES

Please see Item 1, PREVIOUS DESCRIPTION OF MY SERVICES. Given the recent changes in our organization, you agree to onboard 50% of my services without asking me too many follow-up questions thereby causing me to reabsorb said services out of sheer frustration ("Are You Kidding Me With This"). The exceptions to this updated division of services are: 1) emotional support and 2) spiritual support, which are now being reallocated in full to our Infant. I, of course, will still be in charge of blow jobs but at a frequency that will require a separate agreement and also a calendar ("Yes This is Depressing").

4. PRIVACY

There is none.

5. ACCEPTANCE OF TERMS

You understand by continuing to use my services you may be exposed to workplace hazards such as heavy sighs, scattershot memory recall, frequent disappointment, and hormonal swings that frankly will be terrifying for us both. I reserve the right to ignore ("Not Take the Bait") the same behavior from you, which will have no physical nor hormonal basis whatsoever. Further, I will label offensive any statements I deem inaccurate. For example, referring to "our pregnancy" or "our labor" would fall under the latter category. It is your sole responsibility to navigate this process through a series of informed guesses ("Reading the Room").

6. INTELLECTUAL PROPERTY RIGHTS

You agree cute stories about our organization's newest member represent joint intellectual property and, as such, you are not allowed to just go ahead and tell these stories without first saying something like, "Okay if I tell this one?"

7. NO WARRANTY

I OFFER NO WARRANTY ABOUT MY SERVICES, INCLUDING ANY REPRESENTATION THAT MY SERVICES WILL BE UNINTERRUPTED, ERROR-FREE, OR DELIVERED WITHOUT SWEARING OR PASSIVE AGGRESSIVE COMMENTARY. ALL SERVICES ARE PROVIDED ON AN

"AS IS" AND "AS AVAILABLE" BASIS AND ALSO APPAR-
ENTLY IN ALL CAPS. FURTHER, I DO NOT WARRANT
THAT ANY ISSUES THAT ARISE WITH MY SERVICES
WILL BE CORRECTED, PROMPTLY OR OTHERWISE.
OH WELL.

8. RIGHTS YOU GRANT ME

By talking with or at me you grant me the worldwide, nonexclusive, royalty-free license to copy, adapt, modify, display, and
otherwise find a variety of novel ways to complain ceaselessly in
multiple forums, including but not restricted to "nights out with
friends" and Twitter. If these complaints get back to you, you
agree to feel personally attacked and make a sustained shrugging
motion like that John Travolta *Pulp Fiction* GIF. If you behave
in this way I will agree to disagree and say something like, "Just
know someone else feels personally attacked every single day in
this organization. Me, from the waist down and tits up." This will
forever be known as the Nothing's Fair, No One Wins, Everyone
Loses phase of our organization. We will probably laugh about
this someday ("We Will Not").

9. ENDING THIS AGREEMENT

You may end your agreement with me at any time by deactivat-
ing your personality and discontinuing your use of my services.
And I do mean all of them. Please be aware if you just *threaten*
to end your agreement with me, it should be sufficient for a
good 3–5 years of soul-searching and doesn't cost a thing. See
(4) PRIVACY for more information on what will happen to your
personal information when you end this agreement.

10. FEEDBACK

If you choose to provide input and suggestions regarding problems with or proposed modifications or improvements to my services you hereby grant me ("This Bitch") an unrestricted, perpetual, irrevocable, nonexclusive, fully paid, royalty-free right to exploit the feedback in any manner and for any purpose and no shit word-for-word this is actual legal language I only had to insert This Bitch into.

11. ECOSYSTEM OF SERVICES

The modern world requires me to use the term "ecosystem" in all but the relevant and accurate ways. Ecosystem.

Everybody Wants Some

We did not agree on how much sex we should be having.

And we talked about it, rarely.

We did not agree on how much alcohol we should be drinking.

And we talked about it, occasionally.

I learned about sex the same way most teenagers in the '80s did, by doing and not talking. But obviously, unlike most teenagers, I also worked in a porn shop. Whatever non-porn information I stumbled across was either clinical or unreliable and contained double standards galore. What I also learned was that sex and alcohol went together like peanut butter and jelly.

Alcohol bonds well with multiple behaviors, as anyone who has ever enjoyed a drink can tell you. Smoking. Doing drugs. Taking chances. Online shopping. If you are prone to overthinking or simply want a reprieve from the daily pain of being alive then alcohol truly is the ticket. Socially acceptable. Readily available. Two big thumbs up. 10 out of 10, would recommend.

It bonded us from the start, it facilitated our sex life, it made managing small children more tolerable, and it greased the wheels at parties. Alcohol, above all else, is immediate and temporary. It helps you feel better until it doesn't. It feels innocent and fun until it's not. And it's easier and faster than just about any other solution available.

This isn't a confession nor is it a story of addiction and redemption. This also isn't a typical middle-aged tale of recreational deprivation or the American need to pathologize anything that feels good. It's about how we each decide what matters to us alone, once we are partnered. It's about all the hills we maybe should've died on but thought it might be easier to just pretend those hills didn't exist at all.

The attempted talks about sex. The actual talks about alcohol. Instead of judging for myself what was important, I unwittingly judged the outcome of these interactions based on how Jon felt. If he didn't seem bothered, then I accepted I shouldn't be bothered either. Somewhere along the way (can't imagine where except everywhere) I had absorbed the idea that if The Man was happy then The Woman should be, too. I mean! I would've never, ever articulated it in those exact terms and neither would he. We both would've been offended by the mere implication.

But I realized—eventually—this dynamic was a bit of a relief. Because when I'd bring all of this up, wringing my hands over what these sometimes mismatching wants or occasionally concerning habits meant for Our Future, and he'd respond, "This is just what I thought it would be like at this stage" or "I don't think it's that big of a deal" I would feel like, oh! This is just *my* problem! Oh, good, it's just in *my head*. Oh, thank God, this is just *me* not being *satisfied* with how things are. *Problem solved.*

Sometimes I'd even admonish myself, was I looking for trouble? Didn't we all have bigger fish to fry? If things were good enough, good grief, what was I even complaining about? Oh *did I want my life to be perfect?* Oh *do I want absolutely everything now?* Didn't I know there were children starving in Africa? Didn't I know some women were beaten every day of their lives? Didn't I know there were children starving in America, too?

Sex and alcohol are big things. But I had also compromised on small things without ever being asked to. Jon is not a dancer but I was. *Was.* I lived for a club, a party, all the possibilities. We did dance at our wedding, to "The Best Is Yet to Come," after taking dance lessons to ensure we wouldn't rock back and forth with one another like middle schoolers on opposite sides of the same mirror. Once a week we learned to dance to that one specific song, him stepping on my feet, me laughing, his mother dying, the worst deciding to come first. We missed our last two lessons when he flew home to Alaska to be with her.

I'm not sure how often we danced together after that. Probably a slow song here or there at a wedding. I stopped dancing because he didn't dance and something that I thought was temporary or perhaps a demonstration of my dedication to our relationship turned into years of not doing something I loved. Then we had kids and who the hell is going out dancing when they've got babies? Certainly not me, a mother and a suddenly serious person who no longer has time for the simple joys of being alive, thank you very much!

Years passed and I'd be at a wedding or a party and I'd discover the hard way I no longer knew how to dance. I would realize it right there on the dance floor, not remembering where my arms or legs went. I felt old and self-conscious, not wanting to feel like someone's *mom* even though I was, in fact, someone's actual mom.

Jon had never asked me to stop dancing, of course. I had made that decision all on my own. I had decided to stop doing something I loved then resented him whenever I would be sitting there, a wallflower. Maybe I assumed these were the qualities that would make me good in the long run. Sacrifice. Loyalty.

I assumed however much drinking we were doing was fine

as long as the other person agreed. I assumed whatever sex we were having was the correct amount according to marriage and phases. Whenever we'd hit streaks, less drinking or more sex (never both at the same time), I'd consider us fixed through the simple magic of not having said a word.

When we were first married, we would go on tears.

Entire summer weekends spent in the sun listening to Radiohead. Ducking into our house to have sex in the middle of the afternoon, just like that. Lounging in a plastic kiddie pool on our deck, smoking cigarettes, with a cooler full of beer as a side table. We would talk, but I have no idea about what now. I think the silences felt different then, too. I remember thinking, *how could anyone think marriage was hard? Give me a break.*

We were happy and it was easy and the sex was probably enough and alcohol had helped us do all of that, hadn't it? Is that so bad? If we went out to eat and didn't talk all that much, who cared? We got the ups-and-downs life had promised and we weren't struggling-struggling, you know?

We had enough, I kept telling myself.

We had enough, and maybe we should just drink to that.

We had enough, how could I be so greedy as to want more?

Must be nice to want more.

How to Fix Your Hedonic Treadmill

Have you thought about just not getting on?

Have you consulted the owner's manual, which does not exist?

Has it seemed erratic and a little jerky? If so, your hedonic tread-mill is operating correctly.

Have you observed it day-after-day and created a laundry list of all the things that are wrong with it?

Have you tried unplugging it then plugging it back in?

Have you noticed a slipping sensation? You realize that's what treadmills do, right? They sort of do a slipping thing, moving you farther and farther away from where you want to be unless you rush to keep up? Anyway, this is also considered operationally normal.

Have you tried taking all your crap off it first?

Is your hedonic treadmill operating exactly as expected? This is certainly disappointing but also not the treadmill's problem.

Has it shut down without warning? Honestly this is the best out-come possible.

Is the display completely blank? Also a blessing.

Have you noticed a burning smell? Again, normal.

Have you noticed friction, failed circuits, overheating, and/or a need for lubrication? Join the club, hedonic treadmill.

Have you tried getting off it?

Have you considered yoga instead? Yoga fixes everything.

DIY Marriage Therapy

If you think you will find something good, something rewarding, by snooping on your partner's phone I think we all—you, me, your neighbor, your God, an actual houseplant, a cat—know you will not. Our phones contain something worse than our secrets, they contain the truth. What we really say, how we really feel, typed with letters, applied to texts, said off the cuff, sometimes about someone you love for an audience that is definitely not them.

Our phones are the direct and secret lines between friends, confidantes, flirting partners, potential lovers, complete strangers. What used to be a passive object attached to the wall and tethered to a curly cord is now still coiled but alive, a snake. A password figured out, a phone left unlocked, and suddenly you're reading that your husband of twenty-two years called you "high-strung" to someone who was *your* friend first, motherfucker. Maybe you see an unfamiliar name or a heart emoji. Maybe you wonder, just for that flash of a glance, how well you really know the person you're married to.

These are, usually, nothing in the grand scheme of things. Me, high-strung? Well, that is true. I have said more caustic, more intimate things about Jon through my phone but that's not the point. I have flirted and relished mildly suggestive texts from former sex buddies, gladly. These never led anywhere but that's not my point either. My point is phones have the power to crack it all wide open. They have the power to both start and end things.

I can't remember now why I checked his phone that other time, all those years ago. This was barely pre-smartphone, most still dumb.

My memory of what triggered this breach of partner etiquette is lost. I was in our one tiny bathroom, in the first house we owned (does a house you've made fewer than 36 payments on count as "owned"?), our children just two and four years old. That bathroom and its renovation were the source of some of our worst fights, the most mind-bending what-the-fuck-are-you-even-talking-about fights. Even though one of us was a professional carpenter. Even though people did this sort of work on their houses all the time. And no, we didn't have enough money to do it properly. And yes, it would've been him doing it all on his own. And yes, we had two little kids in the midst of their very-little-control-over-their-bathroom-habits stages and it was absolutely the one and only bathroom in the house. But still, that bathroom somehow became one of the most insurmountable obstacles to have ever faced a married couple in modern history.

Anyway. His work pants were crumpled on the floor of that awful, dollhouse-size, ugly-ass, peeling-linoleum-floor bathroom. I reached into his pants pocket and found his phone. And there they were, texts from a woman I did not know. Of course, men innocuously text women and women innocuously text men all the time and the world keeps spinning on its axis. This wasn't that. I knew this wasn't that. As anyone who has been through this can confirm, this leads to an inevitable and frenzied cascade of clandestine tasks all performed while your face burns. You go ahead and act in bad faith because, you suddenly realize, you have been treated in bad faith.

I logged into his Facebook account because this is just how transparent we had been with each other. *I was the one who set up his account, I was the one who urged him to join Facebook in the first place*, I remembered as I checked his chat history. He never changed his password. Why would he? He never lied about anything. As far as I knew anyway. Not until now.

And there she was. My hands were shaking as I absorbed the lightness, the flirtiness of these exchanges, the precise coordination of their phone calls timed for that space between him leaving work and him coming home—back to me, back to us. I wanted to smash the phone and Facebook and the entire universe into a million grains of sand. I began to connect the dots that whatever *this* was, it began when he was out of town. While I took care of his children (they were now *his* children, in my rage). They were so little then, it was so much work. All these years later I remember we drove to Joe's Snack Bar in Jericho to get creemees. I was eating a butterscotch sundae while I looked up, admiring how green the leaves were, unfurling into the hot blue sky after the long winter. And I remember calling him to see how his trip was going.

Turns out it was going fucking great.

I assumed it would be me. Had I not cheated on every boyfriend I had ever had? Well, if I didn't I certainly thought about it. Had my mother-in-law not promised my father that her son would never hurt his daughter? He was to be the good guy, me the bad. This was our unspoken path.

And if I'm being honest, it felt like it was only a matter of time. I didn't trust myself at all because I didn't have a history of trustworthy behavior. Yes, I was in love with Jon, absolutely and completely, but I also had no comprehension of what I had signed up for when I signed up for marriage. I had absorbed the idea I should want marriage more than anything. So, I did. I wanted it. More than anything.

I remember being in a hotel elevator with a freelance producer after a post-shoot tour of bar after bar after bar concluded with us all being poured into a cab. It would've taken absolutely nothing for one move to be made and for that move to be accepted. I had been married for one year. One. But nothing happened and I woke up relieved, as if it was all completely out of my hands. I was just over here, with no power over my actions apparently, leaving it all to the fates.

I remember all the times since when I wished something would happen. But I never made a single move, I never said a single word. I did not love him any less, but maybe I would never be loved enough by him or anyone. Maybe it just wasn't possible then, maybe it's not possible now. Or—honestly, why *woe-is-me* read even that much into it—maybe I just wanted to have more sex? Fuck it. I have been trained by a lifetime as a girl, an adolescent, a woman to frame everything using the handy and acceptable construction of love and relationships. So palatable, so pure. God forbid it could be more primal than that. Jeez Louise.

There were all the times a look lingered just a beat too long. A hug pressed a little deeper than I might've expected, then I pressed back as if to say, "Oh, okay, that's how it's gonna be, huh? Here are my ribs, baby." That hot breath in my ear as a kiss grazed my cheek at the tippy tail end of a party, saying our goodbyes. These moments would never hold up in either a court of law or public opinion. These moments make us feel alive. Do I Still Got It or What? We all have those moments, so don't act surprised.

The work husbands and other people's husbands. The guy at the coffee shop and on your commute. The one from all those years ago and the one from five minutes ago. That one across the room, this one right here on Instagram where I end up down a rabbit hole looking up his ex-wife and his adult kids and I'm like, yeah, that works. The one who paid attention to me, really paid attention to me, the one I could talk to for hours. Nothing happens. Nothing ever happens. I never stop to ask myself why I keep searching. I just accept that I do.

There was that one time I sat across from someone I had come to realize I was in love with and I probably had been since the day we met. We were at lunch, in the middle of a snowstorm, the first few sips of beer slowly snaking their way through my body and warming it. I honest-to-God thought I would burst into tears, I felt overwhelmed at this realization, happening in the middle of a boring restaurant on an unassuming Wednesday or Thursday. Because what did it matter? We were trapped inside our own lives. We had made *commitments*. We had *responsibilities*. We were just on this *slow, boring march* called *life with children*. But maybe I shouldn't speak for other people.

We were talking about nothing, nothing at all, but I remember thinking, God*damn* it. I am fucking in love with you. Shit. I shifted my gaze to the windows, to the snow swirling around outside, a light and beautiful tornado. I had to. I felt dizzy. I felt alive. It felt pointless. I remember thinking this moment, utterly mundane from the outside, was magical. Ugh, gross. I couldn't deny how cozy it all was. It was cozy and it was magical and I couldn't believe I was being forced to think these barfy words but what could I do? They were accurate. I remember feeling, in my gut, this was not completely one-sided.

I remember this still.

But nothing was said.

Nothing has ever been said, on any level or in any way.

And this tiny lopsided emotional affair isn't why I'm getting a divorce.

But this is the answer people want.

The truth is infinitely more boring.

I never cheated. Not once, not ever, not even a kiss, not in twenty-five years. It was just a story I had believed about myself. In *Miss Americana*, Taylor Swift talks about how stars can become stuck at the age when they became famous. I have come to believe the same thing about the age when you get married. Whatever you believed about yourself then is what you will continue to believe for years and decades to come. Unless something—or someone—shows up to change your mind.

It's quite something to expect to be the sinner and instead turn out to be the saint.

The texts. Back to the texts. I finally confronted him.

I don't remember specifically what I asked but I do remember he lied. As we looked at each other I felt the darkness closing in from the corners like a vignette, the feeling you have before it all goes black. I can still conjure the heat in my face, the stunned look on his. I had so often been told how lucky I was to have found Jon, how lucky I was that he loved me. In that moment I thought, *look at the man who everyone told me I didn't deserve.* But even in being caught, he hadn't done anything, really.

This woman was someone he had known his whole life, but didn't have an ongoing relationship with, not even a friendship. But one trip had changed that, when they saw each other again. And suddenly someone was paying attention to him and being nice to him and telling him how handsome he was. How could anyone resist that when things aren't going well? How could anyone resist that when your marriage is in its most trying phase yet? Overwhelmed by the intense need to simply survive having young children. An absence of the tenderness and consideration you had started out with. A vanishing view of the land your marriage had been founded on. Time will not heal these wounds, but this is what you assume.

Anyway, it's asking a lot. They were drinking and talking and likely both thrilled by that combination of familiarity and attraction. Everything old is new again, indeed. And once he returned home that conversation and connection had spilled over into texts and phone calls. It had spilled over into real life.

After he told me everything (I accepted that it was everything, maybe I didn't really want to know), I tried to understand what had even happened. I told him I would be emailing this woman and I did. I warned the woman who had been texting *my* husband and having long phone conversations with *my* husband and who had spent a nice long night at a bar drinking with *my* husband (isn't it easier to frame it as who has possession of the ball? Isn't it all easier to view as a stranger's fault?) I would track her own husband the fuck down. And I would tell him what she'd been up to on her own dumb phone if she ever tried to get in touch with my husband again. Mine, mine, mine.

The "everything" he told me amounted to nothing in the big picture, but that didn't mean it meant nothing. When we ask, "what happened?" in a scenario like this we are demanding a play-by-play. We want to know where hands and mouths and private parts were. We want to know who did what to whom (do we?). We want to know, after the physical tally, was there love? Well, that's what I wanted to know anyway.

But what if none of that happened at all? What if the true

transgression was revealing our brokenness as a couple instead of anyone else's bodies? What if we were already so far gone we just weren't really even all that nice to each other anymore? What if we had lost the most basic and polite levels of respect for each other through the process of having and raising children, keeping a household afloat, arguing over fucking bathroom remodels? What if he felt an ongoing level of loss and grief in his own life—both parents now gone—that I didn't even understand, that I never thought to ask about, because I was so committed to my own story about what was and wasn't working? What if I assumed a person who smiled a lot was absolutely fine? What if my entire emotional response system had been built around the "squeaky wheel gets the grease" and I had married an efficient and silent wheel? What if he thought I had everything I needed? What if we just never talked enough to find out?

What if everyone around us assumes we're happy?

I tried to figure out what to do, where to go next.

We were sufficiently freaked out.

Our kids were still little, so little.

I couldn't believe this was happening to us, the couple who seemed to have it so easy.

I felt like we were smart people who could figure this out.

I also felt like we couldn't afford therapy.

This would be a mistake.

I proposed we do our marriage therapy ourselves. Us, two people who had just skirted the edges of infidelity and whose lack of communication and connection had brought us to this place of marital implosion. Us two noncommunicating dipshits were going to do this ourselves.

Great idea.

Me, King Dipshit, likened this intrusion into our marriage to an infection. A foreign body had permeated the vulnerable membrane of our relationship, attacking it, filling it with pus. I singlehandedly decided the only thing to do was to take a scalpel (words) and drain the wound (our relationship) of everything infecting it (every honest or negative or sad thought we'd ever had about our marriage or each other).

We spent a week on this exercise. The instructions (that I made up based on nothing) were to just get it all out on the table. Write down everything we had ever wanted to say. What was hurting us. How we really felt. Be as brutally honest as we could. Somewhere along the way I had absorbed the belief that absolute transparency and 100% honesty were how successful marriages worked, along with sleeping in the same bed and having a joint checking account. The goal was obviously to meld into the same organism over time, the same heart, the same brain. Now was the time for that honesty, now was the time to meld. I thought we would only have to do this once in our lifetimes. We would feel relieved. We would heal. This would fix everything.

Instead, when we sat down on the couch and faced each other in that first house we had bought together, where we brought our daughter home from the hospital and our children shared a bedroom, where our elderly dogs lived their last days and we threw birthday parties and hired the music teacher from their preschool to do a sing-along, we managed to inject a truly staggering amount of poison directly into the body of our marriage.

We did not do this through insults. There was no name-calling. Neither of us even raised our voices. We did this in the most devastating way possible. We told the truth. We told entirely too much of it. I, of course, hadn't realized such a thing was even possible. How could it be bad to share your most intimate thoughts and feelings? How could it hurt to be honest?

That honesty sliced through everything like a deep paper cut—fast, surprising, barely visible to the naked eye. And, because we knew we were both being honest, we would never be able to take any of it back.

Not only could we not afford marriage therapy but we couldn't afford to go out on dates. But I decided one of our first steps in salvaging this relationship was to get back to being in the actual relationship. I felt like I needed to come up with a solution, preferably one that didn't require paying a babysitter. I decided to be scrappy. Who needed money? Our kids were little and once they were in bed, the night was completely ours. Instead of sinking into our separate worlds as we had been, I decided every other weekend we'd have a date night at home.

I, I, I. Up to that point it was always me doing the thinking. I knew that, but somehow I still didn't realize it. My ideas, my agenda, my concerns, my preferences, my plan. This included the infrequent dates we had gone on since our kids were born; me identifying the need to go on a date in the first place, my suggestion of what we should do, my securing of a babysitter, my designating the time we should leave the house. I realized this needed to change, yet even as I was figuring that out, it was still *me* figuring that out.

We alternated what we'd do for each date night and the other person had to go along with it. It was all very innocuous, it's not like either of us was suggesting hunting women for sport or anything. He chose playing a board game together one week, I chose drawing blind contour portraits of each other the next. I realized, as we worked on our portraits, that we never just looked at each other anymore. We barked, we grunted, we moved on, rarely meeting each other's eyes. That exercise of holding a constant and focused gaze felt physically painful. Still, it softened us.

The portrait I drew of him still hangs on the wall of our living room, twelve years later. I think it captures him well, but there is a dull pain I feel when I look at it. I remember sitting on that couch and how scared we both were yet there we were anyway, drawing one another. It's the same with the photos of our family from that summer, at the beach just down the road from our house, our daughter opening her birthday presents in the backyard, at the 4th of July parade in Richmond. Every time I come across those images I think, *that was the summer. Look how hard we are trying to seem fine.*

The dates helped and him being in charge of half of them helped, but it was not enough. We had tried, we really had tried. But we were amateurs and we had created a professional-grade problem. So we finally called in a professional. Money be damned.

We ended up, as in every scene out of a movie, on a couch together sitting side by side, facing a therapist who was every therapist in Vermont. Brown and gray tufts of hair on his head where hair could still find purchase. A sweater vest. I had seen three therapists in my life, all in Vermont, all briefly, all wearing some variation of that vest. He had a bushy mustache that reminded me of my US History teacher in high school. He had a kind and mellow disposition, which, of course he did.

I started off by telling him what had brought us there. How it started. (It had obviously started earlier than The Incident I keep saying started it all, because of course it had. This mostly innocuous nonevent just gave us a little thing called urgency and another little thing called terror.) He listened, he nodded.

Then I told him how we had attempted to fix it. How we had poured out our every feeling and brutally honest thought, how we had written it all down. On paper. A physical, tangible thing, not a I-think-I-said-this, no-you-didn't-you-said-that situation. How we had exchanged these pieces of paper as if they were holy gifts instead of bombs with the fuses already lit. And how we watched the other person read our honest words, knowing they were honest, and then witnessed as they were diminished by all that honesty.

If he could've gotten away with it, I suspect he would've let out a long slow whistle. Because his first response was, "You did *what*." No question mark.

Me: "Yeah."

Him: "Wow."

We sat there for a few beats. No one said a thing.

When he came to, he told us we had been bold and brave, we had had a conversation that people who'd been married much longer than us had never had. I felt proud of us in that moment. We had done something no one else had done! I look back now and think, *and no one else ever should*.

I don't remember how many more times we went back to him. It wasn't many. Maybe two or three. I don't remember what either of us got out of it, other than the solid concept of having an objective third-party mediate conversations with your partner. Because in nonmediated, nonobjective-third-party life, one person will often dominate the narrative and make most of the decisions. One person will set the social agenda, pick the city, buy the concert tickets. One person will tell you what you think, not overtly (but sometimes, yes, overtly). One person will tell you who We hate now and who We like now and who We will be hanging out with more. One person will have some sort of control the other person doesn't have and who else but an objective third party is going to be like, "Hold on a minute."

Nobody likes to think they're not in control of their own lives as an adult person with agency. But ask yourself who's in your circle of friends and how exactly did they get there? Whose family do you spend the most time with and why? How did you come to live in that house, why are those sheets the sheets you both sleep on? Why that dog? Why that car? Why this school district?

Maybe it is not this lopsided. Maybe you have Big 50/50 Even Steven Energy. But just for kicks, ask yourself how did you really get to all those final decisions? The weekend plan? That vacation? That rug? Your life? We each exert power where we can, without even knowing that's what we're doing. We want proof you love us. And if you loved us you would agree with us most of all.

But maybe you are too in it to tell. Or too in it to care. Or you know what? This works just fine for you. Let the other person figure your life out for you. Who gives a shit? Let them tell you what to wear, where to show up, what to do when you get there. Let them lay your life out before you, like a suit on a bed. Because to be honest you hadn't given it all that much thought. Let them do it. Let them do everything. And when they are struggling, when they feel alone and lonely, when they don't even know what the point is anymore, when being the decider is no longer enough, let them decide what to do about that, too.

Let it be their fault.

Let them do it all.

For a time, therapy scared us straight. We bounced back. Losing my job helped. We again had a common enemy. The importance of common enemies in a marriage cannot be overstated. We pulled together, he cheered me on. I ended up making more money than I did before, almost immediately. We could afford all the therapy in the world if we wanted it. But neither of us wanted it. He hated it and I didn't love it. And I trusted we would somehow, as if it was an organic and inevitable process, be fine.

We never talked about that chapter again.

We never talked about much of anything.

If you have thought throughout, *Texts? A conversation in a bar? Phone calls? That's it?* or *But nothing even happened!* you are missing the point. It is rarely the big things that kill a marriage. It is the little things that whisper to us, "You aren't in love anymore" or "Are you happy?" or "What the fuck are you two even doing?" but you refuse to listen. Because this is not how it was supposed to be.

We wrote so much in those notes. I know I still have them somewhere but I haven't been able to find them (believe me, I have tried). I know they're tucked into the same black sketchbook we had used for our portraits because whenever I used to come across it, I'd see those pages sticking out, and I'd move it along like it was on fire.

I don't remember most of what we wrote to each other. I know those notes were longer than any love letters we had ever written, but that doesn't mean they were lengthy. They contained honest complaints, large and small. But I do remember we each said exactly one thing that's never left me.

He told me I made him feel stupid, like he was lesser than. That when he was texting with this woman and talking with this woman it was nice—for a change—to feel like someone cared about what he had to say or complimented him on anything at all. I made him feel small, constantly. And I told him that when our son was only a few weeks old, I was holding him in the kitchen of our rented farmhouse, my hand cradling the back of his round baby head as I gently swayed back and forth. In that moment I felt the weight of his tiny body against my shoulder and breast, and I looked over to Jon and thought, *I have everything I need now. I don't need you anymore.* I hadn't willed this thought into existence and I was horrified by it. I was so happy then, where could this have come from? It felt like ice water draining down into every chamber of my heart. Even as I calmly kissed my baby's head and rocked him, a scene that would've seemed wholesome from the outside, this happy little family. Suddenly, my love had limits.

Our DIY therapy, like our marriage, had been entered into with the absolute best of intentions. But I realized too late that the complete and devastating truth does not bond people back together. Instead it creates scar tissue, sometimes making it impossible for the wound to heal smoothly, for the scar to fade neatly over time.

For a long while afterward I felt angry with myself and embarrassed I had come up with such a brutal and cockamamie scheme. But perhaps I should feel proud instead, proud of both of us, for having given it a shot. Proud of us for being willing to try. Because eventually we would stop trying completely. Eventually neither of us wanted to know.

Contempt, and Other Things
Familiarity Breeds

- Pandemics
- Inside jokes
- Children
- Inside jokes about pandemics and children
- The same bed, for some reason
- Ability to conjure whole worlds with vague phrases like "did you get the thing at the place" and "you know, the whatsit"
- Ability to agree to leave a boring party simply by making eye contact then motioning with your head toward the door in a diagonal half nod
- Ability to repeatedly "not see" extremely obvious things you don't feel like dealing with like cat barf, a sink full of dirty dishes, wholesale marital implosion
- Camping, for some reason
- Selective hearing
- Selective caring
- Selective swearing
- Whole-hog acceptance of theme park pricing structures
- I-statements instead of you-statements
- Just your basic garden variety silence
- Road trips that will be "so fun, you guys"

- The absolute violence of human chewing and breathing sounds
- Dishwasher loading turf wars
- Toilet seat protocols
- Custody battles over a comforter that isn't even all that great
- Encyclopedic knowledge of historical familial slights
- Encyclopedic knowledge of buttons easily pushed
- Encyclopedic knowledge of condiment preferences
- Love, sometimes, somehow, for some reason

Funny Story

Let's place ourselves at a party. Let's consider the flow of the conversation. Let's pause and begin, "Funny story . . ." Our partner suddenly tunes in, wondering which story this might be. Is it a good one, a light one? Is it funny for both of you?

A funny story is a seemingly innocuous way of bringing others into your relationship. Without necessarily intending to, you are telling them who has the power and who does not. You are demonstrating who is allowed to tell the story of your life together. Depending on the story, the listener believes they're getting a true window into who's a good sport, who's just so very funny, and which one of you is absolutely throwing the other under the bus right now.

The funny story I'm about to tell you is ours. I have told it often and it always delivers. But in the telling there is, as with so many funny stories shaped for public consumption, much that is missing. This is the type of funny story that answered an innocent question that never felt anything but loaded to me. Because the only way to answer the question without sounding like a horrible person was to make it funny. Fermenting something less-than-flattering into comedy is a time-honored coping mechanism, because it works. So I used this funny story to make light of a fucked-up situation of my own making that came at the expense of a person who always trusted me, always took the path of least resistance, and who would've loved to have been consulted on the trajectory of his own life once in a while.

Friends who had seen the photos would ask but mostly state, "So you got a dog." This would lead to a forced laugh from Jon, "Oh yeah, we got a dog alright. Tell them." That would be my cue to jump in with my top hat and tap shoes and tell the story. Otherwise it would be an uncomfortable anecdote of an answer. A presentation of facts where, if I were to be completely honest and add no humor whatsoever, it would cause the listener to react as if they suddenly remembered they had something in the oven.

Funny stories are a sugar glaze. Because you can't ask your fellow partygoer or dinner party attendee or mutual friend if they want to hear a why-my-partner-gave-up-long-ago story or you'll-never-guess-what-an-inconsiderate-witch-I-am story or this-marriage-is-in-complete-failure-mode story. As you might suspect, those stories tend not to be people pleasers. But with a funny story, the bitterness slides down their gullets, leaving a smile and a little buzz. No aftertaste.

This is marriage as public performance.

This is our funny story.

Getting a dog is not a funny story or even a particularly interesting one to anyone other than dog people. Dog people want more details about a new dog than new grandparents want about their first grandchild. What is there to say about a baby? Name, weight, length, and honestly that last one is kind of a throwaway. How long is a baby supposed to be, anyway? It's not a fish. And obviously there's "gender," if that hasn't already been ruined by a reveal involving silly string, smoke cannons, a piñata, a car burning out with pink or blue smoke pouring from its tires, an accidental wildfire, or the fact gender is a social construct based on sex parts and now kills people at parties where they perish surrounded by streamers and cake.

The thing is, I had spent years trying to convince friends not to adopt a dog, especially if they had babies or were hoping to have them soon. I'd tell anyone who would listen that a dog invites a level of work and chaos you absolutely cannot anticipate. And if you already had little kids, a dog was not a substitute for that "just one more kid" you'd never be having. And the kids you did have were not going to help with the dog no matter what they said! The whole thing was a web of lies! That just as things were getting easier was not the time to make them harder again. Why do people love to complain about how hard their lives are then seek out novel ways of making them harder still? I was here to save them from themselves. I was here to warn them, like The Ghost of Dog Owner Future.

I was speaking from painful experience. When our kids were little—newborns, babies, barely over the toddler threshold—we had two elderly dogs. Our oldest dog, Lula, flooded with anxiety when she was left alone, which, unfortunately, was often. She'd attempt to scratch her way through our wood floors and would successfully gnaw on the door jambs. Sometimes she shit all over the living room whenever I was running late getting home. I would throw open the front door, racing to release her, and our big doofy black lab mix, Sammy, would sit in the corner like, *Girl, I did not do any of this.*

We started taking them to dog daycare to save our security deposit. We couldn't afford it, but a house we did not own was being destroyed and we couldn't afford that either. We were being stretched unbelievably thin, emotionally, physically, and financially. We were both working full time and had two little kids in daycare, the financial relief of public kindergarten still a ways off. Aside from small incremental raises, more money would not be coming our way. We couldn't afford these dogs. We couldn't afford the stress. Out of desperation, between the two of us, a hushed suggestion was made to put them down. But I knew I couldn't afford the guilt either.

They roamed the kitchen floor like furry catfish, vacuuming up every dropped Cheerio, every tossed tater tot. Sammy sat at the kids' feet, always protective, always loyal. Lula had had it with everyone. It had just been the two of us back in LA, where I adopted her the day after someone tried to break into my ground floor apartment as I slept. Then in rapid succession I had added a man, another dog, then two small humans. She got bumped further and further down the love and attention totem pole. First slowly, then entirely, she retreated into her age.

Because she was the oldest, we had expected her to go first. But an emergency call from dog daycare, telling us Sammy appeared to be going into shock, disrupted our world order. Lula, less than a month later, declined rapidly over the course of just a handful of days. She went from being able to stand and walk on her own to being unable to do either, Jon having to carry her out in the backyard to pee. I still have a photo of him in the dusky early morning light, holding her and attempting to navigate his way down our rickety back porch stairs. Within one summer month both dogs would be gone.

Ultimately these had been my dogs. I had made the decision to adopt them. I had also made, in ways big and small, a daily choice to neglect them. I went to work, stayed late, and in a variety of ways pushed the responsibility for what I didn't want to do onto Jon. Picking up dog shit in three different yards from

Portland to Vermont, cleaning up warm dog vomit, fixing the damage they had done to every one of our houses, walking them in torrential Oregon downpours. The actual literal shit work of pet ownership. I had been like a child, wanting only the good parts, the easy parts for myself. And he accepted this over and over again. He rarely said to me what we would one day say to our kids, "You wanted a dog so badly, you can help take care of it."

After they were gone, we were free to just be the parents of children. We felt relieved. We were *those* dog owners. We had dogs, then we didn't have them, those loyal companions, and we were relieved they were dead. No more dog food to buy, no more kennels to reserve, no more dog daycare to pay for, no more houses to destroy. No more wondering what that bump or lump was under their fur and how much it might cost. No more having to rush home after work, we stopped rushing home after work. No more picking up puke as fast as possible, before it soaked through paper towels and onto our bare hands. No more dog farts. No more guilt most of all.

We were done.

We agreed, no more dogs.

Never another dog.

The funny thing about window shopping at the humane society—which is how we ended up with Sammy back in Portland, just a little trip to "take a look"—is I had learned nothing. I thought because I was looking online and not in person that that didn't count as a window at all. Even though they were called windows, right on my computer. "Open a new window in Chrome." Duh, dummy, duh duh doy.

My daughter had created a daily ritual called "Can we look at the Humane Society?" which meant bringing up the website for the local shelter and looking through all the very good photos of the very good boys and very good girls that were available for adoption. My daughter had three mice then, on purpose. During one of our quick scrolls through the website we saw Rosie, a peach-colored mouse. She had come in with another mouse but that mouse had died. Now she was all alone. My daughter asked if we could go take a look at her.

We ended up with a fourth mouse.

Four days later we ended up with a dog.

This is, finally, the beginning of the funny story.

This is a story about how we swore we would never get a dog again. I leave out the parts about the neglect and the guilt, me stroking our old dogs' heads as they slipped away from us. I leave out the condolence cards sent from the veterinarian's office and dog daycare. I leave out how we felt broken by having old dogs and young kids and the easiest creatures to blame in that scenario were the dogs because what could they say? They were dogs and they were dead. We had prided ourselves on never being *those* people, the people who viewed dogs as starter children. We would never be the kind of awful people who would toss their dogs over in favor of babies.

And we didn't. Technically, we did not. But I think we lost some of our humanity in trying to keep four vulnerable creatures alive simultaneously. In our funny story I don't share how I began to hate dogs, hated having dogs near me at work, how presumptuous that all was. Not everyone likes dogs! I didn't want to pet dogs or even look at dogs. I didn't want to smell them or have to interact with them or have them wiping their drool across my pants. I couldn't believe I had ever loved dogs at all. And no I didn't want to hear your dumb story about your dumb dog. Jesus Christ, boring.

But then I saw her photo. And this dog was gorgeous and sleek and looked just like Lula but with stripes. She was Lula 2.0 and sure that's creepy, but we all have our types. I can't keep track of all the people I know who ended up marrying someone who looked more or less like their ex and I'm like, wow okay, so this is a template situation. Fine.

Jon and I were not in the habit of effectively communicating with one another generally speaking and by that point in our marriage I had learned I could pretty much just make whatever decisions I wanted to make. So I casually commented, as if I was announcing a trip to the market to pick up milk, "I'm going to look at a dog." What I didn't say is *I had already looked at a dog.* And not only had I already looked at a dog, I had put a deposit down on a dog, now that you mention it. Well, okay fine, a non-refundable deposit if you want to get all specific about it.

Unlike me, a person who is angry for no reason practically all the time, I had only seen Jon angry maybe half a dozen times in my life. He has been annoyed, sure. Outraged when the grocery store rearranges its layout, absolutely. But genuinely mad at *me*? So rare even now I'm having a tough time placing those exact moments. But I was greedy and wanted the generous easy-going guy who was going to say, "A dog! That's great!" but that is not what happened. He was mad and could I blame him? If the roles were reversed I would've burned our house to the ground just so that dog wouldn't have a place to live. I would be outraged by this break in our pact. To riff on *Seinfeld*, anyone can just *make* a pact. The key was to *honor* the pact. And our pact was: no more dogs, never another dog. It wasn't like he hated dogs. That wasn't the issue. He just knew which way the shit flowed on Pet Ownership Mountain and it was directly downhill, pooling right at his feet.

I handled it like I was handling everything else in our

marriage. I ignored him and just did what I wanted to do anyway. I asked the kids if they wanted to go meet a dog and given they'd been asking for a dog for almost eight years they lost their minds. I asked Jon if he wanted to come meet her and he flatly responded, "no" and turned away.

God, he was pissed. I felt queasy and ashamed. But certainly not queasy and ashamed enough to reconsider what I was doing. I wanted this dog more than I wanted him to not be mad at me. I wanted what I wanted and if other people didn't want what I wanted, well, that was a "you problem" not a "me problem."

The funny story. I know, I know. I'm getting there.

The kids and I went to meet her. Jon, giving in, arrived to meet her, too. But it was with the resignation of a man on death row. He had seen this movie before. He knew how it ended. We went home afterward to discuss it. This was the most performative part of our marriage. Rarely did we "discuss" anything. I presented my argument, the counter arguments, and then I came to a conclusion that was obviously in alignment with what I had wanted all along. He usually sat there and listened, sometimes sighing. This was just how it had unfolded over all these years, me in a relationship more or less with myself.

But this time was different. For the first time, possibly in our entire marriage, he exploded. He knew I was, once again, about to be that child who wanted what she wanted until she didn't want it anymore. Then it would become his problem. And he wasn't wrong, not wrong whatsoever. *If you get this dog, I am not taking caring of it*, he yelled at me. (He never yelled at me). And, the same way a child might respond, I yelled back, *Fine, she'll be my dog. She'll only be my dog.* I said it with as much cross-armed pouty-lipped defiance as you're imagining right now.

Fine, she would be my dog.

Neither of us had any idea how true that would turn out to be.

The first night she cowered in the hallway, afraid of the open spaces in our house, especially the kitchen. If she wasn't stuck to my side like static cling then she was in her crate. The morning after we got her I looked down at her, spoke to her gently, and she looked up and smiled. She fucking smiled. When dogs smile it's disconcerting because it looks like they're baring their teeth (well, technically, that's what a smile is) and I looked at her and said, "Did you smile?" and she flashed her teeth slightly again.

Holy shit you guys, we've got ourselves a smiling dog.

She had come with the name Sadie but as everyone knows you can't have a dog named after people you know, no matter how tangentially. For 24 hours she was Coco. But that didn't feel right either. My kids got off the bus from school, racing in to see their (my) new dog and I said, "She's not Coco. She's Edie." If she was going to be my dog then by God she would have an appropriately batty name. Little Edie Beale Harrington.

She's my dog. She's my dog. She's my dog. He's not going to help you with this dog, I had to tell myself over and over again. When she whined in her crate at 2 a.m. and 5 a.m. When she stole LEGOs and pens and socks. *She's mine, not his. She's mine, not his.* This prayer of responsibility forced me to realize how much I had foisted on him throughout our marriage and how much he had accepted without complaint. I didn't want this anymore, I don't like this, this is yucky, here you do it. But this was a standoff of the highest order and I could not cave. I would take care of this fucking dog if it killed me.

Instead of killing me, it cracked me open.

I found: What the sky looked like at 5:30 a.m. How enchanting our neighborhood felt on December nights, snow blanketing every surface, the moon illuminating it while white and candy-colored lights peeked and blinked from windows and trees. I noticed which households put their Christmas trees up first and which two were the last to take them down in February, even though they didn't have kids. I loved that detail most of all. I discovered there were woods and paths behind our neighborhood and the hill we had repeatedly scrambled down during a neighborhood cleanup three years before was the same hill where most of our neighbors took their dogs to shit. I now said it casually like, "Oh you mean Dog Shit Hill?" I knew where all the best flowering trees were in the spring, the most brilliant leaves in fall. I felt a special appreciation for neighbors who planted lots of tulips and wildflowers. I was in awe of the canopy of crows that engulfed our neighborhood every November, the owls haunting branches and power lines in summer, and rabbits and chipmunks that would take over completely in the spring. I watched a searing shooting star as it aimed for the horizon at 4:15 a.m. I looked up, often. To pink clouds and constellations, building thunderheads and blizzards. I rediscovered what it was like to be outside often, breathing fresh air, whether I wanted to be doing that or not.

And I began to write. If I was up at 2 a.m. or 3 a.m. or 4 a.m. to deal with a whining pup then I might as well stay up and do something. This is how I started writing again, for the first time since I was in my twenties. I would take Edie out, then turn on the tiniest pool of light and make coffee. I'd curl into a recliner and wrap a blanket around my legs. And there she would be, curled into a tight little donut beside me, her velvet ears within reach when I needed that soft reassurance. This would be a heartwarming story, a real *awww* kind of story, except for what I haven't told you yet.

It turned out Edie hated men. This is the funny story. How we got a dog we said we'd never get, a dog Jon definitely did not want, and punch line: *Turns out she hated men.*

Ha. Ha.

Not only was she *my* dog but I had immediately become *her* person. I couldn't leave a room and go into another room without her hot on my heels. She was ready to defend the house against all potential intruders—the mail lady, the FedEx guy, the UPS man. Anyone who came into our house who was not one of my children. And especially, especially, men. Big, deep voices, beards, hats, heavy boots. Who knows why.

Now Jon had a dog he didn't want, living inside his house, sleeping and whining in a crate in his own bedroom. A dog that would growl and bark at him no matter where he went in the house. He stole my response, something I often said to him when he'd startle when I simply walked into a room—"I live here!"

At obedience class I asked what to do about this whole man-hating situation and I returned with handouts and tips. At one point Jon agreed to walk through our house with his pockets full of cut-up cheese and hot dogs ready to funnel into Edie's mouth, to bribe her into liking him. Insult to injury doesn't begin to cover it.

It took not months, but years, for her to accept him more fully. These days I'll return from a long walk with her and if Jon has just pulled into the driveway or is out working in the yard or playing basketball with the kids she will see him and wag her tail. Lately she will do more, straining against her leash and bounding toward him, genuinely.

I think she thinks she won.

We make fun of Edie for all the things she's afraid of. Paper bags, not having a completely clear path between the door and the bed, the kitchen floor. But how funny is it, really? She's afraid of something dumb. We're all afraid of something dumb. When she curls up next to me, her body presses hard against my leg even though we're on a queen bed and there is plenty of room. Her proximity to me akin to what one might experience on a life raft. This is what makes her feel okay.

I am trying to feel okay. I am trying to accept that although I am a fundamentally good person with a guilty conscience, I am also a bit of an unrepentant asshole. I am trying harder to recognize when I make light of someone else's pain or shirk my own responsibilities, candy coating them with humor. Sometimes a funny story is nothing more than a funny story. And sometimes it's the violinist on the *Titanic*, giving you another place to focus your attention, up high, as the disaster unfolds under the surface.

Storytellers fill their narratives with inciting incidents. What Joseph Campbell referred to as "a call to adventure." These moments set stories in motion. A sudden desire. A secret agenda. A decision to neglect. A decision to fight back. Life, death, life, death, over and over again until you can't believe how often it keeps coming up. A smiling creature, hot dogs in a pants pocket. Defiance. Forgiveness. Acceptance.

Funny, isn't it?

And You May Ask Yourself, Well, How Did I Get Here?

Let's try a little experiment:

Step 1: Choose Your Favorite Person

Step 2: No, Really

Choose this person regardless of their gender or sexuality, or yours. Your only focus right now should be the whole "favorite person" thing. Choose someone you can spend an enormous amount of time with, just about every day really. When something happens, they're the first person you want to tell. And they're the last person you want to talk to before you drop off to sleep. You love and value them. You can't imagine your life without them.

Step 3: Share Some Common Interests

Some of their interests should overlap with yours in a way that bonds you, creating a world the two of you can share. Sense of humor, self-righteous belief in your joint superiority, owl figurines, you catch my drift. You can certainly learn from or even take on one of their interests and vice versa but you shouldn't count on it.

Step 4: Live Together

Congratulations, you live together now! I know this seems sudden but no point in dillydallying. Clock's ticking! You share the same kitchen, the same toilet, the same refrigerator, and the same address. And oh, the art. That reminds me.

Step 5: Decorate Together

Since you live together now you also decorate your home together now. If you have similar taste in decorating that would help. Not having an opinion? Ideal. Because whose art will be hung on the walls? What about paint colors? Do you care about backsplashes? Wow this really is a whole thing isn't it? But whose thing is it anyway? Have fun!

Step 6: Eat the Same Meals

You now eat meals together, the same meal. This is the expectation. Obviously you can *snack* on whatever you want. But snacking is different than meals, especially dinner meals. Did you always eat the same dinner as, say, your college roommates? No? Well that's over now. You and your favorite person eat the same thing almost every night, together. Because guess what, that's how this works. If you don't eat the same meal, people will write articles about the dangers of making different meals. Just watch. Yum-yum!

Step 7: Watch the Same Shows

You now watch TV shows together. Don't worry, you don't have to like them the same, but you do have to watch them simultaneously. How dare you watch something on your own or before your favorite person has had the chance to catch up or—worst of all—without even thinking of them at all? What are you, some kind of monster?

Step 8: Combine All Your Money

What?!?!! Yes. Combine all of it. Doesn't matter whether you make more or they make more or neither of you make any. It's both of yours now. Do you share the same beliefs about money? Do your spending habits match? Odds are they sure don't! Whoops. Our sense of self-worth is all twisted up in money and look, here you are. Surprise! You probably haven't thought about why you handle money the way you do until now, while all your money is busy having intercourse with someone else's money. Do you hoard it? Spend it? Well, combine it anyway. Good luck!

Step 9: Sleep in the Same Bed

Jesus. I know. On top of all that other togetherness and TV show syncing and food matching and money intercourse you now also have to sleep in the same bed. Light sleeper? Late to bed, early to rise? Early to bed, late to rise? Late to hell, early to God please kill me? Okay, well, you'll need to sort that out. Nighty-night!

Step 10: Have Jobs and Ambition

Difficult to say whether it's better to have the same level of ambition, different levels of ambition, the same level of ambition but at different times, or different levels of ambition but at the same time. But you should probably figure that part out unless one or both of you are the beneficiaries of generational wealth and, if so, I look forward to reading all about the launch of your twee and unnecessary brand of whatever in the Style section of the *New York Times*!

Step 11: Get an Additional Family for Some Reason

Even though you already have a family, guess what, now you have *another one*. Like one per lifetime wasn't enough! You now carry familial grudges for your favorite person or adore their various family members according to an abundance of one-sided information. Their family is now your family even though you will *not* just get to say whatever you want to them and yes, I know this was not in your original calculations (see Step 1) whatsoever. Bit of a scam, isn't it?

Step 12: Be Young

Forgot to mention this earlier. Be young when you pick your favorite person. Like, really don't know what the hell to expect going forward. If you are old and also picked an old person, sorry, you know too much. Go back to Step 1 and start over.

Step 13: Make Some People Together

Look, don't get hung up on the logistics. The most important part is you've chosen your favorite person. SO IGNORE THE LOGISTICS FOR NOW, I CAN'T STRESS THIS ENOUGH. We will ratchet up the level of difficulty (I know! This was already getting kind of hard!) with a defenseless infant who needs 100 percent of (someone's) involvement to keep them alive and safe. This small human child will eventually share just about everything you had previously only shared with your favorite person, like food and the TV and probably the bed, but brain and heart space most of all. You'll figure it out. Somehow. Won't you?

Step 14: Keep Getting Older Together

Are you changing? Is your favorite person changing? Do you want different things? Are you just bored? Imagine your best friend from high school or your twenties. Could you have lived with that person this long doing all these things? The sleeping in the same bed, combining all your money, and figuring out where the art goes? Not bloody likely, right? Anyway! Keep getting older with your favorite person, the person you never had a single doubt about at the beginning of this experiment. You didn't doubt them, you didn't doubt yourself. Back then your time together could be described as "effortless." Seems so long ago now, doesn't it?

Step 15: Do It

Here we go. Now imagine on top of all this (that's what he said), this person must be someone you want to have sex with and they want to have sex with you. For years on end until you're horizontal for good they should be fulfilling all your sexual needs as you should be fulfilling all of theirs. Or will they? Or will you? You'll have to talk about that. Or do you? Let me introduce you to the lifelong campaign of sexual misinformation, fucked-up silence, and unnecessary shame called Growing Up in America. Do you like the same things in bed? How will you know? Do you have the same sex drives whatsoever? Let's let those small people you made chime in. They want to sleep in your bed, too! Everything is fine. *That's what no one said.*

Step 16: Face It

Seems like we sure expect a lot out of marriage, don't we? Seems like it's almost, dare I say, completely fucking unrealistic? Feel free to go back through and add your own categories, the expectations you didn't even know you had, and the pressures and internal dialogue that led you from one step to the next with almost no critical thought whatsoever. Seems to me we should be more surprised when two people make it all the way to the end of this little experiment than when they don't. You know?

"DIVORCE"

Insanity is doing the same thing over and over again and expecting different adults.

—*September 15, 2020, 51 years old*

Lightbulbs

1.

Six years ago.

It was a birthday party, my birthday party. By far the fanciest birthday party I will ever have in my life. I invented the party because I needed to justify spending $2,000 at a charity auction for a weekend stay at a circa 1840 forty-room farmhouse, even though Jon's truck had needed new snow tires for a year.

Only my little family, just the four of us, had stayed in that mammoth estate the night before, needing walkie-talkies to communicate between the wings. But that night it would be a party for twenty, the maximum allowed. My friends had planned the menu and rushed through the heavy front door, in from the late afternoon sun and dazzling mid-October day, with bags of groceries, armloads of flowers, wardrobe changes. It felt like preparing for a state dinner.

I did my makeup with a heavy hand, for the first time grasping that it wasn't the fix it had always been. Instead of helping, it was hurting, holding up for a few minutes and then, suddenly, ruining me. I applied more, surely more was the answer, but instead it just made me look old and crazy. I wiped it off and would need to start again, and this threw me. I shifted gears, slipping my black sequined shirt dress with the silver bugle-beaded collar over my head, smoothing the lining down, tugging, adjusting.

Jon and I had claimed the master bedroom with the attached screened-in porch, of course. We could claim anything we wanted to that weekend. Jon got dressed, buttoned his shirt, tied his tie. There was no flirting or teasing. There wasn't a light touch on a cheek or hands pulling hips closer or nuzzling into a neck. There were no allusions to what would happen in that bed later, because nothing would happen in that bed later. This time in our marriage was neither antagonistic nor angry, it just was.

He went downstairs to get a beer and grab a glass of red wine for me as I sat at the vanity, attempting to rejigger my makeup strategy. I had learned long ago not to panic when makeup application before a big event wasn't going as I had envisioned. Just take a breath, do something else for a minute, start again. I adjusted my collar and put on my shoes. Then I dabbed on concealer. Conceal, conceal, conceal. I was alone and felt alone, suddenly more alone than I had remembered feeling in a long time.

Then I thought it and saw it as sure and clear as if Jenny Holzer had projected it onto the mirror I was facing:

I need to get a divorce.

2.

Four years ago.

These talks had started a few years before this—five years before, actually. Almost as if on a schedule, they would repeat every three years, then more frequently, every year. Pressure would build. Unhappiness would overwhelm. I would state that we needed to talk. I would ask, "Should we get a divorce?" Then he would say no, that this is just what he thought marriage was supposed to be like during this stage, that he was happy enough. And this always worked for me. I never questioned it. I needed the release of getting everything off my chest and I would mistake this release for resolution.

In the middle of one of these talks, in the middle of what had become a predictable pattern—me flipping out and crying, him reassuring me that he thought things were fine, this was just a phase, me talking in circles until I tired myself out, me feeling relieved, both of us exhausted—it finally, finally hit me. My face, already stained with tears, suddenly became still. My voice, calm.

"You're never going to leave me, are you? No matter how unhappy you are. No matter how miserable you might be. No matter how bad this marriage ever gets. You will never pull the trigger, will you? You are never, ever going to be the one to leave."

"No. Probably not."

3.

Two years ago.

We always used to say we were so lucky to have met when we did. This was our destiny narrative. We met at just the right time, in just the right place, at just the right age. I would always joke that if we had met in college we would've hated each other. I can't imagine my wearing-all-black, smoking-cigarettes-while-wearing-dark-red-lipstick, cynical, pessimistic self could've tolerated for one single second the slightly stoned, very chill, happy-to-be-alive, smiling, skateboarding optimist that he was. And most certainly, vice versa. It had become a bit of an inside joke, a comforting story, between us.

But during the year when we were the only ones who knew we were getting a divorce I said, "What if that story was all wrong? What if we met during the *only* window when we would've gotten along? The *only* time we would've fallen in love with one another? What if it wasn't destiny at all, what if it was just timing? Can you honestly say that if you met me at a party right now that you'd think we'd make a great couple? That you'd fall in love with me? Do you think you'd look across the room and think we were meant to be together?"

"No."

"Me neither."

How to Punch Your Kids in the Face

This is where my mind instinctively went during these particular conversations. Divorce conversations. The first time one of us brought it up (it was me), the first time we stared at each other and thought (I thought), "Is this what we're really talking about? Is this what it's all come to?" and also, "Why aren't you having any sort of big reaction to this?" I was mostly, if not completely, thinking about my kids.

I would picture them asleep in their beds, soft light illuminating their faces and blankets tucked in just so, like a Lifetime movie about divorce. I imagined this even as they got older, even when they were long past the ages of their blankets being tucked in just so. Still, in my mind, they'd be enjoying the deep sleep of the unbothered. Their faces smooth from their short years and lack of worry. They had their beds and their books. They had posters and photos on their walls, things they liked to look at. They had each other. What else was there?

I pushed myself, for years, to believe the same thing. We had each other. What else was there? Couldn't good enough just be good enough? Wanting to be happy was selfish. For women.

So I would decide, as I thought of them, I couldn't do it. We couldn't do it. (And why was it up to me?) I decided I would rather stay together forever, like a test of endurance, than detonate their happy lives. I would seethe, in some of these go-nowhere-arguments, "I would rather be miserable every single day for the rest of my fucking life than hurt them." And Jon would nod, sadly, agreeing. Neither of us were monsters and that much we agreed on. But we weren't in love either. This wasn't working and hadn't worked in a long time and I was the only one bringing it up. It was easy to keep going when I weighed "This is fine. So I'm a little unhappy?" against "Potential emotional damage to the two people I loved most."

But "the rest of my life" had a different ring to it as the years went on. For one thing, I got older, as the living tend to do. And for another, people around me started dropping dead. Not to an alarming degree but to a degree that said, "This is only the beginning." Those people had plans, they had vacations right around the corner, their kids were still in school, they thought they could do things differently, fix their mistakes, make their lives better, just later. Then, gone.

But even more than my own mortality, my kids were getting older, as kids also tend to do. They were transitioning from being little kids who couldn't possibly understand the complexities of a marriage to teenagers who were learning—by example, just a little bit each day—what to expect from a relationship. This was one of the switches that finally flipped. After years of hemming and hawing, approaching the brink and backing away, it came down to one simple question: Did I want them to learn about marriage from this marriage?

Did I want them to think: Marriage is never holding hands or a surprise arm snaked around a waist, pulling you in close? To think "not horrible but not wonderful" is a benchmark? To believe an administrative, project-managed existence was something to aim for? Did I want them to commit to a life that was security, devoid of passion? Did I want them to carry forward a template of snippy little comments like, "Can I talk to you in the other room?" Or the pervasive feeling of *is this it?* Of caring just a little bit less each year? Well, did I?

We were demonstrating every day, to our children, that marriage—this marriage anyway, the marriage most pertinent to them, the marriage that got them both here—was no longer about emotional intensity or basic curiosity or true connection. It was an agreement to endure. We were teaching them that sometimes marriage was nothing more than a socially approved grudge match.

So I made the decision. I was finally done. And Jon accepted it. This was not exactly a new conversation or an unexpected outcome, but it says more than enough that he didn't push back, didn't ask what we could do to save it, didn't say anything really. He didn't even show any emotion, only crying when he started making calls to tell other people. In the moments when it might've mattered, he didn't cry to me or over me or over us, he saved it for someone else. That still pisses me off.

But it was done. Well, for us it was done. It was just starting for everyone else, including our kids. The fear of this moment, the moment of telling them, had almost singlehandedly kept us married. But it was finally here. Almost.

Because of the truly unbelievable things that happened to delay the news—throwing a 20th anniversary party for a marriage we had agreed to end, publishing a book centered on motherhood where I barely talked about our marriage and when pushed by my editor to write more about it I instead wrote a conceptual essay after responding, "I'm all done writing about my marriage in this book"—it took months to set a date to tell our children.

Our kids were in middle school. They weren't overly scheduled but they were not not-scheduled either. We needed an open weekend; we needed runway. We turned down every social obligation only to find a field trip here, a game there, a dance that weekend, a birthday party the other weekend, something torpedoing every single date we picked.

Our kids went trick-or-treating without us because they were no longer little. We took that opportunity to sit down at our dining room table. We lit the candles and drank the wine and attempted again to pick a date. Our friends and neighbors were out with their own kids trick-or-treating and they'd been drinking. I missed that phase of trick-or-treating when it was an excuse for an open container jaunt around the neighborhood.

Their kids ran up to our front door and we deposited fistfuls of candy in their pillowcases and jack-o'-lanterns and cloth bags. Our friends thought it'd be funny to leave their empties with us, and I have never been less in the mood to clean up empties in my entire life. It wasn't their fault, of course. I couldn't wait until everyone knew so we could stop having to act like everything was so very funny and so very cool.

They texted us later, inviting us to come over, have a drink, have some soup. Then the next text said something along the lines of, *unless this is alone time for you two if you catch my drift.* And wow was my laugh about as bitter as bitter gets as I looked into that glowing screen.

The following week I met my aunt Janet for lunch in Manchester, New Hampshire, the halfway point between my home in Vermont and hers in Rhode Island. While I explained what was looming, the family meeting that would end it all in less than two weeks, the world outside was engulfed in gloom. The concrete sky had cracked open with a cold rain that assaulted, so cold, in fact, it was a shock it wasn't snow.

While we were talking and I was crying and we both drank a middle-of-the-day glass of wine, I intentionally let the parking meter lapse. I knew if I ventured outside to feed the meter, even if I ran as fast as I could, I'd end up soaked down to my underpants and chilled to the bone for the two-and-a-half-hour drive back. The sheer level of potential misery and ominous symbolism of that day was, if I'm being honest, a bit much.

I told her, "I feel like I've set a date to punch my kids in the face."

I told her, "Every time I talk to him or hug her, I think about everything I know that they don't. It feels dishonest."

When I finally returned to my car after our lunch, with my puffy face and red-rimmed eyes, soaked from the short walk just as I had expected, I of course had a parking ticket. It was hot pink and wheat pasted to my windshield by the rain. I peeled it off, placed it flat on the passenger seat to dry. The twenty bucks was more than worth it.

Maybe caring less was my destiny.

I continued to put numbers to it—in twelve days I will punch them in the face. In a week, in three days, tomorrow morning around 9:30. I felt sick. I couldn't fathom how much I had sacrificed to keep them protected, to keep them free from hurt throughout their lives. Turned out, I was the wolf inside the house all along.

At one point I fooled myself into believing they knew, because children were so perceptive! I leaned into that old chestnut hard. Jon did, too. He even said, without me bringing it up first, "Maybe they already know?" and I found this immensely comforting. Maybe this family meeting would be nothing more than a formality.

They were rightfully suspicious that our weekend calendar was comprised of two completely empty squares, back in the days when that was considered unusual. Jon typically woke up at 9 a.m. on weekend mornings and our son, ever the monitor of inconsistency, remarked at 8:45, "Wow, Dad's awake. That never happens." I just replied with a forced casualness, "Hmm!"

We called a family meeting once everyone was fed and coffee had been made. The kids were down in the basement playing ping-pong together, which seemed to almost never happen anymore. Even though we had waited weeks, months, a year, really, I loathed calling them up and away from their game. I willed my voice not to crack.

"Guys! Come up! We're having a family meeting."

I bowed my head and took my place on our whale of a modular sofa that filled up half the room. The future was now. I had no interest in doing this. I wanted to do this so badly. I hated this. I wanted this over. There was no scenario where they didn't remember this moment and our exact words forever. Honestly, *fuck this.*

I said, "Come on in. Let's have a meeting. We have something to tell you."

And as they bounded in, my daughter, always with her big bright eyes and her voice lifting, asked, "Is it good news?" As it turned out, she coldcocked me first.

I never saw it coming.

I knew I would lead this conversation because that's what twenty-plus years of this relationship had taught me. We didn't even discuss in advance what we were going to tell them. I thought about this constantly. *Shouldn't we discuss what we're going to tell them?* But just on principle I was so tired of being the one on deck when it came to molding the emotional lives of our children. Instead, I would wing it. I couldn't wait to be out of the business of this back and forth, the weighing and the deciding.

With no preparation and no talking points agreed upon, I just said it.

"Dad and I are separating."

The impact.

The recoil.

I felt the trauma pass through them like a sound wave, squiggly, sudden.

In their shock, they reacted in ways as individual as they were. He: Coiled in on himself, the long legs he got from his great-grandmother Nan suddenly pulled into his chest as he turned onto his side. He hid his face. She: Her face flushed red, her soft cheeks burning, her eyes suddenly brimming with tears. In contrast to his hiding, she locked eyes with me and never wavered.

I hated myself.

I hated everyone except them.

I hated the world, I hated love, I hated every stupid failure that had brought us to that moment. I hated marriage most of all.

This is what I told them: First of all, nothing was going to change for a long while. This relaxed everyone. It was also self-serving. This was the whole reason we were able to go forward with this decision at all. Neither one of us could bear to move out. Neither one of us could bear to be away from them. We thought, maybe this is where an absence of fiery emotions would finally pay off for us.

They were growing fast, lanky and curvy; they were becoming adults right before our eyes. Some days it felt like we were growing seedlings indoors, the slightest bit of sun, a dribble of water and *boom*. They reached up, outgrowing everything around them, eating up the sky.

I told them we loved and respected one another as friends, and we were pretty good at being parents together. But we were not in love, and that part was important in a marriage. We were not setting a good example of what a good marriage should be.

We recognized that might not make sense to them now but I told them one day it would (I hoped).

I told them no one loved them more than we did. That every single decision we made going forward would have them at the center. That we were committed to staying in this house together for as long as that worked. That for now, things would seem mostly the same. But the difference was now they knew. And soon, everyone would.

The four of us talked for less than an hour, which surprised me. I had set aside forty-eight hours and we only needed one. I was originally going to treat this news like some sort of fucked-up holiday where nobody did chores or homework, a free-for-all. Sort of like when my own parents got divorced and I got to eat all the sugary cereal I wanted.

But in that moment I decided, after my son asked, "What are we actually doing this weekend?" that this was normal now. I needed to treat this as normal. And I said, "Well like any other weekend, you need to do your chores first. And your homework."

Cue the expected groans.

I could hardly believe how right that decision felt.

This was normal now.

At the end of that hour, as things were clearly winding down, I asked for any more questions or worries to be shared. My daughter asked if we could go out for ice cream and my son announced, "I have four things to say." I held my breath as he continued, "And three of them are about darts."

I heard about all the near bull's-eyes he had made down in the basement before they started playing ping-pong. And I thought, after all these weeks and months and years, that what had felt to me like a punch waiting to be released, was instead a near bull's-eye. We all came close enough.

It counted.

Hi, We're Getting a Divorce

I wrote an email on behalf of Jon and I, presented here without edits. It was sent to our families and close friends first. Some on that list were aware this news was coming or had been told via phone not long before. But most who received it came to this announcement cold. A pared down version was shared with a longer list of acquaintances and family, possibly a hundred people total. A digital carpet-bombing.

As I read the original longer message now, with the benefit of time and distance, I can see I was employing my nascent op-ed skills. I'm presenting my argument, the supporting evidence, a temporary solution, while working to cut off counterarguments. I tried to anticipate questions and answer them.

I was explicit about our point of view as well as the conversations I for one would and would not engage in. No doubt there were countless conversations behind our backs (of course there were), but I can say without hesitation this email allowed us to avoid almost every unpleasant cliché associated with announcing a divorce. It was a proactive media strategy made personal. Going to the tabloid before it comes for you. Maybe it was too honest, maybe it was too much. But then again, it worked.

Hello all,

Some of you have known this news was coming, but most of you do not. I apologize for dropping this on you via email but this is a little easier on my/our emotions than making 50 phone calls and telling this story over and over again.

The personal news is: Jon and I are separating.

Although it's natural to look for the one thing that causes a breakup, I assure you it was not one thing. It was not a festering argument or me writing a book or one specific thing either one of us did. Not that we owe anyone an explanation but searching for a "why" is a pretty reasonable reaction. Even if this feels sudden to you, I assure you it is not sudden to us. We have been discussing this for a very long time. Yes, way before we threw ourselves a 20th anniversary party. There are worse things to do than recognize a big milestone, even when you're fairly certain it will be your last major milestone as a married couple.

We are telling you now in this way because we wanted you to know first. We will share this news more widely soon. We don't want to be in a position of having to tell people over and over again whenever we are out or over the phone (do people still use phones for talking?) or when we're with our kids. Our priority is surrounding them in a web of support and love and because you are on this list, we know you understand.

When anyone has told me that they're getting a divorce, my knee-jerk reaction has always been to respond, "I'm so sorry." This feels like the absolutely natural response. Because news like this never feels like good news. And while this isn't great news, this is also not a tragedy. A relationship has run its course. There are far worse things.

We all spend a lot of time in this life focusing on success and failure. And divorce, by its very nature, seems like a failure. I've been thinking a lot about this (as you might imagine) and honestly what's the failure here? Because it didn't last forever? Many things don't last forever—including our own lives—but they can hardly be automatically characterized as failures. I have been witness to many, many marriages over my lifetime that have continued under what seems to either be a sheer grudge to stick it out or an inability to embrace change. Those are not the happiest people I've ever met. Those relationships do not seem like successes to me, or at least not how I choose to define success. While we can't know what's next, we do know we weren't modeling for our kids what a good marriage should look like. But we have complete faith that we can model what a good partnership looks like. Words cannot begin to express how central our kids are to this decision. Words cannot begin to express how much we love them and how we will do anything and everything to support them.

Jon and I have been through so much in our 22 years together. This decision does not change that. We will always be a part of each other's lives. We will always be family.

You do not need to feel sorry for us. You do not need to whisper or be pouty-lip-sad-face in our presence. You do not need to pray for us or make us feel weird about it or cry on our shoulders (please do not cry on our shoulders). This was not a hasty decision and we are ready to move out of the decision phase and start shaping what our new lives will look like.

We are still great friends who have a lot of love and respect for one another. Because of that, no one is moving out for the time being. God knows we have enough room in this dumb house to give that arrangement a shot. So you can still reach us/send us boxes of money/also singing telegrams to our current address. It took us years to come to this decision so we feel no need to rush this next part.

Most importantly, we both want to spend as much time with our kids as possible. They are growing up fast and our time with them already feels fleeting. We're hoping our non-plate-throwing history will allow us to do this, even during this potentially weird transitional time.

You can still invite both of us to things. You do not need to choose sides (there are no sides). You do not need to be sad for us. What you can do is wish us well as we figure this all out. And if you are close by, you can be happy to see our kids and show them—as you've shown us over the years—that you are the good people we've always known you to be.

With much love,

Kimberly + Jon

I printed out a shorter version, a third version, of this announcement and enclosed it in our holiday card. Yes, we sent out a family holiday card. With us as the band KISS on the cover of *Dynasty*. It was an update of a card we had sent out eight years earlier (our then four-year-old daughter had made a killer Gene Simmons). Back then the inside of the card read A NEW YEAR'S KISS FROM OUR DYNASTY. This time it read ONCE A DYNASTY, ALWAYS A DYNASTY on the left-hand side and on the right-hand side, well, there was this:

> *Even though our band is breaking up,*
> *We won't sit here brokenhearted*
> (sit here brokenhearted)
> *We'll call all our friends in the neighborhood*
> *And get the party started*
> (get the party started)
> *And we'll shout it, shout it, shout it out loud*
> (To back up, by "party" we mean we're fine, don't worry)

Shout it, shout it, shout it out loud

(Wow, really wish KISS had more emotional depth right now)

Shout it, shout it, shout it out loud

(We're a family and always will be, that doesn't really rhyme with anything though)

You got to have a party

(Good lesson here about not caving to peer pressure. You do not "got to have a party")

Shout it, shout it, shout it out loud

(*This is about as far as we can take this whole thing*)

Almost two years later everything about this seems insane to me. All of us sitting around our hefty IKEA dining room table—a table we bought for our first home when we had a two-year-old and a baby on the way, a table with a leaf that anticipated more people at holidays—as we assembly-line-signed over one hundred and fifty cards announcing the implosion of our marriage. I wondered if this wasn't one of the most selfish things I had ever done (I meant the card but, really, the divorce, too). I wondered how my kids were processing this or if they were at all. I wondered what on Earth they would think of this later, looking back on it. Would they think I was making fun of one of the most traumatic things that had happened to them? *Would* they view it as one of the most traumatic things that had happened to them? But somehow it felt right at the time. So many things do.

Did a holiday card using KISS as a delivery device for news of our impending divorce send some people over the edge? I have no doubt. It's a fine line between upending expectations and being cavalier about other people's feelings. I think it's safe to say you could examine that card six ways to Sunday and not find a fine line anywhere in evidence. But what no one tells you about navigating a separation is you're left holding a map that no longer applies. So you have to pick up a blank sheet of paper and start drawing lines somewhere.

As time has gone on, though, I've found myself thinking more about our twentieth anniversary party than the card. I wonder how our family and friends, especially those who were at the party, digested that particular detail. I wonder if they felt tricked or lied to. By the time I told Jon I was done talking about divorce and instead just wanted one, we were already far down the path with the party. We had put down deposits and people had bought plane tickets and reserved hotel rooms. Our invitations were out and what could we possibly give as the reason for canceling? If we canceled the party and announced our divorce it would seem like something sudden and explosive had happened and that couldn't have been further from the truth. I also wanted the party, on some level, to be something of a send-off for our marriage. But others not knowing, that is what I still struggle with most.

That night was wonderful but it was also awkward. I'm not sure there is anything lonelier than feeling awkward with someone you've been married to for twenty years. The gulf between us had seemed manageable inside our own home, but when we were out socially, like getting our portrait taken in front of our families and friends, for instance, it felt like I might drop through the chasm and disappear.

Our friends had assembled a band for the night, playing outside on the patio of the Inn at Shelburne Farms on an outrageously warm October night. When we were beckoned out there, for cake and champagne toasts, they played "Then You Can Tell Me Goodbye" as we sat there together, all eyes on us. If you're not familiar with the song, which I wasn't, it contains the lines "If it don't work out, then you can tell me goodbye" and "If you must go I won't tell you no, just so that we can say we tried."

As the lyrics began to register, I locked eyes with Meg, the drummer, and Amanda, the singer, who also happened to be two of my closest friends and knew the path my marriage was on. I thought, holy shit, talk about a fucking Easter egg.

I sat there in a rocking chair in my beautiful dress holding a glass of champagne and Jon sat in another rocking chair next to me in his suit, looking handsome and happy as always, holding his glass of champagne. The photos later showed people we cared about looking at us with warmth and good cheer. It's difficult to see in those photos how happy our kids were that night. Given how I feel now, if I could go back, I wouldn't have thrown the party. I feel guilty about it, like we were intentionally being deceitful. I feel like we hurt people we loved. But there is also a part of me, when I look through those photos, that feels grateful we had one big night when everyone believed we were happy.

Thank You, Acquaintance, for the Very Good Advice on How to Save My Marriage

This is amazing. What are the odds? Here I was struggling—for years—to navigate the disintegration of one of the most foundational and, dare I say, private relationships of my life. A relationship, in fact, that has lasted almost the entirety of my adulthood. Which is an interesting contrast to my relationship with you, a person whom I have spoken with twice. How I had never thought to consult you, Peripheral Nobody, for advice is beyond me. Thank goodness you are such a warrior for the sanctity of marriage that you stepped boldly over the line of polite discourse to insert yourself into this intimate, intimate area of my life. You are certainly brave and a person who is not reading my social cues right now. Again, I am overcome with gratitude. *Thanks.*

Whew, how lucky am I that you're here? I have been waiting. No one has been offering me advice of any kind on this topic, including suggestions of where I might have failed or interrogating me on what actions I have taken to correct those supposed failures, until now. I was wondering when someone would show up and really get into the weeds with me, a person no one should be doing that with at all. I can't tell you just how relieved I am to see you. And also to hear you talk at me, not pausing whatsoever for my responses, which I can assure you are not forthcoming.

Anyway, can you remind me of your first suggestion? I blacked out with rage there for a minute. Was it, oh what was it called again? It's right on the tip of my tongue. Oh! Was it tHeRaPy? Sorry, never heard of it. No married person ever has. Can you sound it out for me so I'm sure I have the pronunciation right? Can you then spell it for me as well? Is that "therapy" with an "ie"? An "ey"? A whistling smiley face surrounded by one thousand knife emojis? Well, it should be.

Can you, expert resident of Earth and all its many relationships, explain how tHeRaPy works? Hold on, are you *sure* it works? Because I am absolutely in the habit of making sweeping changes to my life based on one (1) conversation with a person whose previous role in my life was briefly meeting near the chips and dip for three and a half minutes at that one party that one time where I said, "Wow, August already" and you said, "Right?"

No, no, you're right, this *is* a tragedy. I don't know how we will survive. Thank you for thinking of my children—whose names you only got half right—and their future intimacy and trust issues. That wasn't uncomfortable at all for you to bring that up. I mean, knock me over with a feather and you with a sledgehammer to the neck, I had never thought of it! But you're right, nothing has ever been worse than this. The world is otherwise a flawless and benevolent place full of relationships that work perfectly forever. We are throwing the whole thing off with our failure, it's true.

But back to you and your monologue. What was the other thing you suggested? Was it having more sex? Communicating? Putting the other person first? Remembering to be curious about one another? Forgiveness? Forgetting? Or was it forgetfulness? Wearing sexy outfits? Journaling? Crying? Lowering my expectations? Performing random acts of kindness? Or at the very least performing fewer random acts of imaginary murder like I'm doing right now? Thinking of our children? Thinking of our parents? Thinking of our vows? Turning to religion? Turning to meditation? Turning to eating chocolate frosting directly from the container? Not blaming each other? Being vulnerable? Exercising together? Not playing the victim? Do you ever get the sense most of this advice is directed at women? Spending more time apart? Spending more time together? Chilling the fuck out? Being more honest but not *too* honest if you catch my drift? Holding hands more? In general, touching one another but also giving one another space? Going on more dates? Shutting down my desire to react? Focusing more on my appearance because Jesus who's going to love me when I look like *this*? Accepting and validating my partner's feelings? Okay, there is just no way men are getting these suggestions. Not comparing my marriage to other people's marriages? Trying to forget everything I know about my marriage and just start over? Date as if from the beginning, which would also require me to act like a person who possesses neither short- nor long-term memory? That should be very easy! Laugh more? Just cool it, you know? Compromise, compromise, compromise? Also, can't emphasize this enough, try to look like a different person? Yeah, all of these are meant for women. Anyway, I will take these many suggestions I have never heard of before under consideration.

Again, thank you for this delightful divorce intervention. Even though my partner and I have come to this decision after years of painstaking work and reflection, I was hoping a chance meeting with someone I barely know while in the salsa section of Trader Joe's would turn things right around. An additional thanks for forever ruining Trader Joe's for me, I will never be coming here again. But you're spot on, this was such a good talk. And again, you're so right, it was wonderful to connect like this— our interaction was definitely not so forced it felt like having my teeth pulled out through my tits.

And yes, I have no doubt you will be soaring on the wings of feeling like a good and superior person for the rest of the day if not your entire life. I'm so glad I could allow you to view me as a failure and you as a success by taking the brave step of second-guessing the actions of two people you barely know. It's people like you who keep the rest of us from assuming all people have the best of intentions. By the way, have you tried their Extra Hot Habanero Ghost Pepper Salsa? Absolutely my favorite and I hope it kills you. Have a great day!

Looking at Strangers

I sat outside a general store in mid-coast Maine on a late September afternoon. It was the sort of late September afternoon people overdress for because it's autumn, after all, there are pumpkins and cornstalks, it is not supposed to be this hot. Anyone who is wearing socks regrets it. They had put socks on that morning without thinking too much about it, as instructed by the calendar.

I had intended to stop by quickly, search for something to eat, and see if they had hot chocolate. Hot chocolate is often attributed to winter but as far as I'm concerned, it's another thing discerning people do in autumn. It's chocolate you can drink, what is the issue?

On my way out I saw the welcoming porch, an empty rocking chair, the sun warm and dappled through the towering maples and oaks. Leaves turning molten, gold, but nothing too flashy. Not yet. Red, white, and blue bunting hung from the rafters. This place was an invitation. This was a place that said, "Where are you hurrying off to, little lady? Sure you don't want to fuck around and fantasize about strangers?"

I *did* want to fuck around and fantasize about strangers. I was supposed to be writing so I couldn't think of anything I wanted to do more in that moment than fuck around and fantasize about strangers. I set everything I had been balancing in my hands down on the bench next to a rocking chair and took a seat. I tried to remember how to operate a rocking chair. Had I even sat in one since I had babies? Am I really this much of an idiot? Does this rocking chair make me look old? I often wonder if the best thing about being dead will be never having another thought again. I found a mellow rhythm with the rocking chair, nothing too showy. Something that said, "I understand how rocking chairs work" and also "but not completely."

I sat there, enjoying the Chamber of Commerce beauty of it all. I realized soon it'd be time to carve pumpkins. I was used to framing everything for the past fifteen years through the lens of my children and their experiences. But with each new season there seemed to be a greater sense of loss, a perpetual state of diminishing returns. Less neediness from my children, less sex in my marriage, less love in my life, less sleep in my nights, less life left to live in general. Less security in my job, less elasticity in my skin, less hair on my head, less hope in my heart. Was I just going to disappear a little bit each year until I finally seared into a pinpoint in the sky?

But I didn't want to think about those things anymore. I thought about them all the time. I thought about them for days that turned into years and now decades. I wanted to think about abundance. I wanted to feel alive. What I'm saying is, I wanted to leer at strangers.

I decided to sit in this wholesome environment with organic grapes and a baguette and a chocolate bar by my side and judge men. I was going to imagine them doing all sorts of things, in various states of undress, in different outfits, as if they were dolls. It would be the grown-up version of those times I sat in my childhood bedroom closet, mashing two plastic dolls together that had been liberated of their outfits while making weird sucking sounds with my mouth.

I had sunglasses on and as I knew from my lifelong experience of being on the other side of this equation, sunglasses are all the equipment this activity required. I was going to imagine these men saying all the things I wanted them to say and also just one hundred percent shutting the fuck up. *This is a world of possibility, this innocent general store*, I thought. *So let's see what's possible.*

In my marriage I had set the bar for what I expected in the sky, among the stars. I needed true partnership, curiosity about my work, clairvoyant physical affection, understanding of modern parenting trends and child development, desire to take over our finances but also let me do whatever the hell I wanted with our money. Total agreement. Emotional alignment. Love.

Funny how far down the list love fell.

"Funny."

And now, from strangers, I wanted much but expected nothing.

If you were driving an old pickup truck and towing a small boat and didn't hesitate a bit about pulling a U-turn in the middle of a country road to park it, that was enough. Did you have Maine license plates? The old kind, the kind with the black letters and numbers banged out of a white background? If you then got out and were tall, had a full head of salt and pepper hair, you were working for me. Did you have a dog waiting in the driver's seat for you to return? Was it a Hollywood dog, perky triangle ears and an attentive face? Are you kidding me? Did I sit there, lingering on the empty truck, the dog, the license plate? Where did you go in that boat? Where are you going next? Did you then

walk back out of the store and look over at me and absentmindedly smile, thinking I was a neighbor? I don't think you were
looking at me at all, if I'm being honest. I think you were just taking in the beauty of the day, feeling the sun on your face. This
was also enough. Were you carrying a baguette and a twelve-
pack of beer? Did you swing the twelve-pack with your tanned
arm and place it into that perfect twelve-pack-shaped spot in the
bed of your truck? Did the handle on your driver's-side door not
even work and you had to reach into the open window and open
it from the inside? That was some teenage-level junk-ass-truck
shit and it was hot. Did I already mention you were towing a
small boat? Am I repeating myself already? Is this a Clint East-
wood movie? Is rural erotica a genre?

I will ignore your Crocs as well as your wedding ring. Both
offensive. Both irrelevant to me and my interests. Take off your
pants.

Why are you driving away?

I spent an hour like this. Looking, imagining, feeling like my
crotch had a pulse. Is this how men felt all the time? If so, I
could officially say, I get it. I finally get it. You are absolute dogs
and now so was I. Is this why you couldn't help but turn your
head when your girlfriend or wife was sitting right there, boring
holes into your thick skull while your cartoon eyes *boing-oing-
oing* toward anonymous tits? How could you not? This was delicious. This took no effort. It was free.

I continued to coolly sift through every man who approached,
picking up the dull rocks and tossing them to the side. What a
relief to not worry about someone else's feelings or think about
their personality or wonder if they're funny, are they generous
with their friends, do they respect their mother, do they find

meaning in their work. Jesus Christ, who cares? This one was too old. Too young. Too, just no, just wrong. This one's pants were awful. What was this guy thinking?

You looked promising. You were not my type at all. You were anonymous and wearing some sort of leather motorcycle racing outfit that would normally trigger my gag reflex a li'l bit. You were riding a type of motorcycle I didn't even like. But you were slender and anonymous. Your helmet was dark and I couldn't see your eyes. I didn't want to see your eyes. I didn't want you to ever take off that helmet. I did not know who you were. I didn't want to know who you were. You could be anyone. You were anyone. You want to know who I was very into these days? *Anyone*.

You took off the helmet. Wow, bad move.

Next.

You were next to me at the takeout counter. You looked over at me a couple times and I kept forgetting, even though it had been almost a year, I was no longer wearing a wedding ring. I forgot this was some sort of signal except when a man I didn't know started chatting me up at a party, I would wonder why this conversation was even happening, then it would dawn on me, oh right, we were absolutely the only two people there without wedding rings. Ugh. Welcome to Loser Town. Population: Us.

Anyway, I looked at your hand and noticed you weren't wearing a ring either. You were good-looking and well put together and had a nice accent I couldn't quite place. You had asked for a half pound of Brussels sprouts salad and then noticed the scale read .7 instead of .5. You did not like this and requested it be .5 exactly. This is why everyone hates tourists. Tourists are such a pain in the ass. They make jokes about how terrible the food is with a self-satisfied smile as they point to their empty plates.

They drink too much in the middle of the day and don't know how to cross the street correctly or in an efficient manner. They talk in accents not your own and you find it intriguing in moments like the one at the takeout counter but then you overhear the fussiness and entitlement and you're like, you know what, I don't have time for this shit. No, you should not be charged more for something you didn't ask for in the first place but for Christ's fucking sake that is a $13 a pound salad you insufferable prig. You're not putting a down payment on a summer house around here with the exactly two Brussels sprouts that were just taken out of that container. Meanwhile the world is burning and I'm horny although I'm not horny because the world is burning. Either way, take your dumb salad and keep walking, buddy.

I wondered how long I was going to have to wait to see someone as good as that first guy. I wanted that first guy to come back and just continuously forget something inside and have to walk back and forth from the store to the truck and his dog as I watched. I wished it was a game where I could choose all the things I wanted to watch him carry to his truck. Even in my leering I had already become monogamous. Even in my leering, I was boring.

Many of the customers, the locals anyway, were at least twenty years older than I was and half of a couple. I wondered if I would ever have that again and then I wondered if I had learned anything at all. I wasn't supposed to be thinking about relationships or love or commitment. Yuck. I wasn't even officially divorced, I was so far away from being officially divorced, and there I was, already getting ahead of myself.

I finally gave up. Not only did I need to get back to writing but I had leered so successfully for so long, both my heart and my crotch were pounding. I drove back on country roads with my hand down my pants like an animal. I suddenly felt empathy for men and the tell of a hard dick pressing against pants. For all anyone knew, I was just a modest lady covered from neck to ankle in olive green clothing for some unknown nonmilitary reason, wearing reasonable flip-flops, sitting in a rocking chair, probably thinking about mulling some cider.

About halfway back to the cottage I took a sharp curve. I always forgot there was a gas station right there. It was that most local of local places, an independently owned gas station. Not part of a chain, hardly any windows. Every time I drove past it I thought, *true crime.*

I looked over and saw the red pickup truck and the dog and the boat. I took my foot off the gas and my car instantly decelerated. What exactly did I think was going to happen? I was not this brave. I wasn't even this weird. I was just a woman who was desperate to feel something again, even if I couldn't identify what that something was. I didn't want to talk, I had done so much talking. I didn't want to compromise or look at a calendar with another human being again for the rest of my life. I didn't want to shuffle the banalities of life back and forth anymore. Life was so boring most days I could scream.

I had no idea what to want anymore. I was so used to thinking in negatives. I had successfully clamped down my emotions and my desire. I had many years to refine this. I had hardened myself in every way possible without even meaning to. It just happened. I had given up. One day I looked around and realized I had no idea how to be a normal person anymore. I had forgotten how to fuck someone. I didn't know how to have conversations that didn't go deep (what was the point?). I wanted to be open while finding a way to do it that involved being completely closed. I wanted more but would definitely settle for less. That's what the last ten years in particular had taught me.

I was tired of looking inside myself for answers. I was ready to be touched. Someone needed to touch me. It needed to happen soon. But I felt like I might shatter if it did. I pressed back down on the pedal and my car lurched.

Off I went.

I was gone.

The Unbelievably Boring but True Tale of Divorce Witch

Gather 'round children, for I shall tell you the frightening and truly tedious story of the scariest of all women, Divorce Witch.

Divorce Witch started out like any other lady. She was a wee baby then a little girl then a slightly older girl but now sexually fair game then an actual woman then married, which made her a princess! She was composed of all the usual lady parts that were constantly being scrutinized for firmness, shape, and size (some were better small and some were better big! But which should be small and which should be big? "Make up your minds!" cried future Divorce Witch!). She had long hair, which was what the menfolk of the village preferred for sex reasons. And townspeople knew that because the menfolk would tell them, constantly, without even being asked for their opinion whatsoever. Like, not asked at all which hair length they thought looked better on the ladies of the town. They would just come right out and say it. Unasked.

Because of this, everyone understood shorthaired ladies were different witches. They didn't care what the menfolk preferred or didn't prefer. They just did what was best for their particular face shape and, you know what, whatever. They didn't have to have a reason. Neither did the longhaired witches. Witches didn't need to justify why they looked the way they looked. Jesus.

Anyway.

One day, although she was very much the same married lady (and therefore a Magical Moral Princess) she got a divorce from the prince (a regular man). Just to review, she was exactly the same lady but now not married and therefore a witch. That's how she became Divorce Witch. Yeah, that was pretty much it. Just, like, instant witch.

Married men—the ones who used to laugh and joke with her and give her hugs—were suddenly wary around her. Would she pull down their pants right in front of their wives? Was she now just a crazed horndog who would stop at nothing to suck off every middle manager and failing creative director in her immediate vicinity? Was she suddenly an insatiable whore who would straddle a pudgy acquaintance triggered by nothing more than a limp handshake? Should they only share greetings with her via a series of fraternity-like fist bumps that ended in a Three Stooges *whoop whoop whoop*?

Divorce Witch had one response to all this tie-clutching, this middle-aged penis-protecting, this self-conscious smoothing of increasingly visible pates. It was a catchphrase that still echoes throughout the land, over the mountains, down the street and take a left, through the water supply, and all up in kitchen faucets throughout the village where future witches would drink it in. And it was thus:

"Ha ha 'Okay dude.'"

Divorce Witch was sick of them. She was sick of everyone. But she knew the men were simple and also somewhat terrified of their wives. Because, lo, although it was no longer 1950, there truly was no one in the village more exhausting than some of the Magical Moral Married Ladies. They were witches at their core but had forgotten their spooky truth. They wore magical rings on one particular finger on their left hand, a finger not all that magically named The Ring Finger. Thus they were made pure and only asked questions heavy on the italics and long on syllables like "How *are* you *dooooing, reallyyyyy?*" and "How *arrrrre* your *kidssssss* holding up?" They thought men were precious, like gold bars or free samples of La Mer. They were also known for greeting Divorce Witch with exaggerated sad faces that made them feel righteous.

Through her many interactions with the townspeople, Divorce Witch discovered she had a mystical power. In the first year of her witchery, she realized she could see the entirety of the inside of the back of her own skull thanks to the many, many times she had rolled her eyes allllll the way back up in there. The inside of her skull was bumpy! And dark!

To the untrained, nonjudgmental eye, she still looked very much like your typical average lady person who's just trying to live her life, man. But to some of the Magical Moral Married Ladies, those lost latent witches, she was something else entirely.

"No! Cast not your lustful eye upon my husband, Divorce Witch!" they'd cry if she even looked in the general zip code of their husbands. And Divorce Witch would think, Bitch, *your husband?* LOL. That guy sucks.

Besides, she had already *had* a husband. What on Earth did they think the point of divorce was? Getting *another* husband? The last thing she needed was another one of those things! Especially a used one! Have some respect ma'am; Divorce Witch was not a Goodwill drive-thru.

One thing Divorce Witch knew for sure? The ladies of the town overestimated how desirable the men they had married actually were. They clutched them closely whenever Divorce Witch was near. At parties, at BBQs, at that thing at school, in the grocery store, just you know, wherever. Because you never knew when Divorce Witch might strike! And by strike I mean just leading her super boring lady life but without a wedding ring on her left hand.

Some people thought Divorce Witch must be incredibly lonely, what with the lack of tedious arguments over who took out the recycling and conversations about "what even *is* this marriage anyway?" But no. That's because Divorce Witch had a coven, as all witches do. Everyone gets all high and mighty about what a coven is and all you have to do is google "coven" and it will tell you a coven is simply "a secret or close-knit group of associates" underneath "a group or gathering of witches who meet regularly." And the former is flagged DEROGATORY! Do you see now what the witches were up against? Lots of people against covens. We don't talk enough about that.

Anyway, the coven understood the raging anti-coven battle that was taking place all around them. But most of all, the coven truly understood Divorce Witch. The coven would say encouraging things like, "Yeah you make a good point" and "Are you going to have any more wine or can I finish the rest?" And although the coven consisted mostly of married ladies, they were the *right* kind of married ladies. They had not forgotten their witch roots. They never spoke in italics. They texted each other knife emojis and drew dicks on photos of things they hated including peppy neighborhood newsletters and Christmas trees they were somehow responsible for taking down without any help from their families. Drawing a dick on a Christmas tree? That's funny.

Eventually Divorce Witch had her own bedroom, as most witches do. She had designed it with pretty wallpaper and a painted floor. There were plenty of books, fresh flowers, two chairs and a little table to set her coffee down upon, and most importantly, no people. When the lady folk of the town gazed upon it, they proclaimed they were absolutely ready to turn gay if they could live with Divorce Witch in her pretty bedroom where men and children were not allowed. They all laughed and laughed! It was almost like the lady folk never had any time to themselves or any space whatsoever! Like, give them a goddamn minute, you know?

The menfolk of the village gazed upon this room then back at their ladies then back at the room and in a low whistle were all like, "Oooooh shit." They did not like their ladies getting ideas.

"Ha ha, too late!" Divorce Witch thought but did not say. She did the vast majority of her talking inside her head, where it was bumpy and dark and italics were used only for excellent comebacks. This whole "room of her own" thing made the menfolk of the village even more suspicious of Divorce Witch. If she didn't want them, well, then clearly she wanted their wives! But, she did not. She didn't want anyone. In fact, if everyone would just stay the fuck away from her that would be fantastic. Dogs were fine, though. Dogs could stay.

The moral of the story is whenever you're out and about in your own village and you come across a Divorce Witch, just remember however sorry you might feel for her, it is likely only matched by how sorry she feels for you.

Later, witches!

The Anglerfish

Phase One: Affirmation

"I could get it."

That is the very first thought I had within five minutes of being on Tinder. This, essentially, had been the question at the heart of every conversation I'd had with my friends and inside my own head since we announced our divorce. Could I still get it? Will I ever feel a dick again? Am I even attractive? Look, I know I'm attractive *enough*, for my age, et cetera, caveats galore, but it was finally dawning on me that the last time I dated was exactly half my lifetime ago. I was that cliché now. I was an about-to-be-divorced middle-aged woman who had forgotten how to date.

The thing was, I didn't even *want* to date. I just didn't. I couldn't even fathom starting all over again when I hadn't even gotten to the end yet. I had zero interest in hearing anyone's life story, God help me. I was long past the stage when I could pretend to be chill, not crazy, and not petty as hell. I was reminded of a story a friend told me, of seeing an extraordinarily handsome man across the bar and thinking, but if I meet him, then I'll have to learn things about him. Like his *name*. This is where I was.

Except: I was lonely. I was emotionally alone and adrift. And I felt trapped. I had agreed to stay in this house with my family

for the greater good. But something was continuing to be sacrificed in that decision. And that something was me. I was still
doing the emotional tending I had done in my marriage and
in our family because what had really changed? The only thing
I was free from was the lie that our marriage was working. But I
wasn't free to just pick up and move out of Vermont—a thing I
couldn't ever fathom having wanted when we first moved here.
This was to be our Last Place. Every day I realized more and
more that, for me anyway, it was just One Place.

I had sacrificed again and again all in the service of my
children's stability and happiness. I was beholden to them like
I promised myself I would be, like I wanted to be. I chose this, I
reminded myself often. No one asked me to do any of this. Not a
single person asked me to do this.

I needed to honor how strongly, deeply they were rooted to
this beautiful, small, unforgiving state. The guilt of moving just
one town over and transferring them to new schools several years
earlier had just about killed me. If the past fifteen years had
taught me anything, it was that the threat of hurting them would
keep me from doing things I wanted to do, jobs I could've only
previously dreamed of, cities where I longed to live, a different
life I desperately wanted to lead. It would keep me in a broken
marriage for far too long. It would hold me in place. My guilt
and my love would form a cage. It would show me what I could
have, but only through the bars, never being allowed to touch it.

Given where I lived and the life stage I was in, I was surrounded by people who had been paired off two-by-two for ages,
like the most boring Noah's Ark ever. I felt like an endling, the
last of its species living out its days in captivity, the only other
route out of middle age being dying. I had to do something. I
would have to travel emotionally, intimately, and in secret.

I decided I either had to give in to dating apps, the only way I could connect with men I didn't know while staying under the radar of my family, or I would end up detonating everything in order to free myself. I had to find a way out of my life without leaving it. This was the only idea I had.

I had started with Bumble. But I realized quickly Bumble didn't have much brand recognition in my rural state. Within an hour, I deleted Bumble. I downloaded Tinder next. I never thought to check with anyone I knew who was actually divorced and living where I lived to see if any of this was a good idea. I was just cruising along on my I-work-in-advertising I'm-on-Twitter I-understand-how-pop-culture-works knowledge, such as it was.

When I opened Tinder, my second thought—after "I could get it"—was *Helloooooo*. This is because I was a dipshit. I didn't realize yet those first faces and profiles were bait. They were bait for people like me who didn't know these good-looking strangers were the veneer of what this app experience would be like. I thought it was solid cherry all the way through, so I paid my money and was suddenly hit with a truly relentless amount of plywood.

I quickly became engulfed in the terror of the swiping and the liking. I swiped right (interested) when I definitely did not want to. I accidentally swiped left (not interested) when I found someone who seemed promising, argh! Suddenly I was a grizzly bear that had just lost a fat salmon in a stream, patting frantically in the blur. Where did he go?? I considered the entire concept of applying a heart to a stranger gross. But clearly not gross enough to stop.

I signed up for the level of service that costs real money because why not? This is what age buys you, being able to see other people's likes on an app that was essentially a people catalog presented inside a glass front rectangle that didn't exist when my children were born.

One thing became obvious immediately. Any man with exceedingly good hair, a delectable sense of style, and who looked like an actual person I might want to kiss with my mouth literally lived in another country. That's what happens when you reside 40 miles from the Canadian border. Almost all their profiles were written in French, a language that I, a person who took three years of high school French and two years of immersive French in college, still did not understand. Had I known, I would've applied myself.

In contrast, let's take a look at the men on Tinder from my rural state. I mentally grouped these men as I swiped through. There were the ones who definitely had at least one body buried on their land. There were the men who were ripped and looked like they said, "Shut up, bitch" on a fairly regular basis. I'd been so thoroughly hung up on whether I was attractive enough and, honestly, I was not the one who was the problem here. What the fuck was this shit? I was paying for access to *this*?

Ill-fitting clothes, shitty apartments, the type of wraparound sunglasses mostly racists wore, and enough baseball caps to choke Fenway. Social media had trained me to investigate the background of photos and I'm sorry, but if you lived in what looked like a hotel room from 1993? That was a swipe left. Haircuts that expired twenty years ago, dad sneakers, aggressive jewelry, eyeglass frames that needed updating. I closed Tinder more than once while whispering to myself, "But why?"

Most of these men, you will not be surprised to hear, did not know their angles.

And then there was the astonishing sameness of the photos. Boats, motorcycles, fish and more fish, so many fish, mountain biking, cars, and God help me, skiing and snowboarding. I had survived seventeen years in Vermont without once seeing snow at an elevation and now this. I had gone hiking maybe three times and that was plenty. One of my most frequent thoughts was *why do I live here?* And the answer was *because I never thought I'd have to date anyone in this let's-go-for-a-kayak, let's-do-hard-things-outside, let's-have-dates-that-require-water-bottles place, that's why.*

There were the ones—few and far between—who had genuinely warm smiles. Their writing was open and witty, they seemed good and fun. But they were not attractive. I was not going to settle for someone less handsome than Jon, what was even the point of that? There were the creative types who wrote conceptual profiles with insane punctuation and formatting. Their photos so intensely edited I might as well have been swiping on a graphic novel. Their bios contained SCHOOL OF HARD KNOCKS for their education and TORTURED ARTIST as their occupation. I imagined a tiny ref on the field, tossing a red flag in the air that read LOOKS LIKE A HANDFUL.

I shuddered at every poorly lit photo of a man with his shirt off, lying in bed. Inexplicably this was too much nudity for me. The ones of almost completely naked men standing in their disgustingly filthy bathroom mirrors, with their faces obscured and their boxer briefs pulled down just shy of Dick Town, earned an out-loud *yikes* as I swiped at the speed of light, trying to unsee. I couldn't begin to wrap my head around what would happen when the first dick pic inevitably arrived. I had never received one before and I was not looking forward to it. Were men aware of what those things actually looked like? Certainly nothing to be proud of.

I thought back to how much smaller I used to make myself

when I was dating. I forgave and looked past a thousand red flags. I felt like I couldn't expect much, I had to seem easygoing and up for anything. I remember one blind date where I was forced to go hiking in the Santa Monica hills and first of all, cliché. Second of all, I was a regular smoker back then and lived the life of a vampire, rarely venturing out into the oppressively optimistic California sun. But I did it. And I hated it. I hated that dude and I hated myself even more. But I was willing to do just about anything to have a shot at being loved. And in order to be loved, I learned early on, I could not be myself. I was too difficult, too demanding, I thought too much, I was too sarcastic. I wasn't pretty enough to receive that sort of leeway, like a blessing. It was a sliding scale after all.

But I just didn't have it in me anymore, I guess. I no longer had the wellspring of compromise I was born with, alongside all the eggs I'd ever contain. So there I was, not wanting to deal with another human man at all, possibly for the rest of my life. I was so fed up with it all. Past. Present. Future.

Unfortunately, they were the ones with all the warm dicks.

Phase Two: Sadness

Fuck, we are all so old. I thought this every time I opened Tinder.

I thought about how most of the people my age on this app, myself included, probably didn't want this. And given the visual evidence, most of us weren't ready. We didn't realize when we cropped a photo the whole photo was still visible on the swipe through so there's your ex-wife and your kids. We didn't realize what we thought was our sexy face was, in fact, our murder or corpse face. Neither were ideal. I read the profile of a man who was not my cup of tea but then I got to the mention of him being a widower and I whispered "oh no." This is absolutely the last place he wanted to be. I felt sad for him, I felt sad for myself, I felt sad for all of us except the guy who wrote in all caps I AM NOT HERE FOR THE NECK UP PHOTOS (although I wholeheartedly agreed).

More than once someone wrote that they were looking for their "last great love" or "last partner" and, well, Jesus. I hadn't really thought of any of this in those terms. "I want to love just one more person and be loved by them in return before I die." I mostly just wanted someone to either feel me up or have a good conversation about books. I wasn't ready for the last of anything yet.

I lowered the upper limit of the age range I was looking for to only four years older than me because for a while there I felt like I was trying to date my dad, eek. I couldn't figure out what was happening to my brain. I looked around at the men I knew and they didn't look as old as these guys did. Then I realized, well, most of them *weren't* as old as these guys. But more importantly, my friends were obviously people I knew. Their intelligence, personalities, humor, all seemed to lighten their ages. Is that how it worked? Is that why we continued to look in the mirror and feel surprised by our own reflection?

I finally texted one of my single friends and told her I had joined Tinder. Immediately a response shot back, Tinder is the grimiest around here and how visceral was your response just now to the word "grimiest"? I grimaced but decided to hang in there, mostly because Tinder already had my forty dollars. She recommended OkCupid. I signed up immediately. I had signed up for three dating apps in three days, which was a lot of dating apps for someone who wasn't interested in actually dating anyone.

I woke up the next morning to 89 likes.

Phase Three: Annoyance

My matches were few and far between. I swiped left on just about everybody because I wanted to know I had options without interacting with any of those options. This was not how people were meant to meet. Or, at least, this was not how I was meant to meet people.

Any man who was fit, seemingly financially secure, and still had hair had it made on these apps. Well, just like they had it made in real life. When I was two hundred miles away from home one weekend, I matched with someone I had swiped right on a couple of weeks before. Who checks a dating app once every two weeks? Someone who can, that's who.

The message from him was as simple as it was annoying. First off, he called me Kim. This had been happening with increasing frequency over the past few years and I did not like it. Was everyone suddenly so put upon that using full names—a name used by me in every possible context, in email signatures, in person, everywhere my name could possibly appear without even a slight variation—was just too much to bear? I decided if I stabbed the next person to call me Kim, I would easily be acquitted by a jury of Elizabeths, Jameses, and Thomases.

Next he wrote, "you're fine but too far away."

I stared at the word "fine." I stared at the whole sentence. Was that fine as in, "Girl, you are *fine*." Or was that fine as in, "I guess you'll do."

I hated this and now I hated him.

I hated everyone.

This was the dumbest thing I had ever done.

But like all the other dumb things I had done, I stuck with it.

Misspellings in profiles were an immediate swipe left. I noticed, over time, there was always one photo that gave away what a man really looked like. I was grateful for the traitor photo. And none of us can know which one of our own photos was the traitor. Swipe, swipe, swipe, oh so *that's* your hairline, swipe left. Swipe, swipe, okay no on the teeth, swipe left. Swipe, swipe, swipe, wow those racist sunglasses again, swipe left.

"Swipe Left on Humanity" would make a good T-shirt.

Phase Four: Masculinity

At the two-week mark, after matches that went nowhere, I was finally matching with handsome men. Before that point I noticed I was sometimes pushing myself to see "beyond" looks, like I had in my twenties. I would love to give a crisp one-hundred-dollar bill to any man I know personally who had ever done this even once in his life, never mind as a matter of course.

I had been narrowing my eyes at bios and trying to analyze photos and judge expressions (would this be the last facial configuration I'd see before he kills me?). But now I was matching with legitimately attractive men who didn't look 49 or 55. Well, they did, but in a way I was accustomed to, the way my own friends looked. After trying to read between the lines of a variety of bios, I had come across one that simply said, 6'2". *Firefighter. Lawyer.* and I was like *that works.*

My friends and I spent so much time going on and on about what we wanted men to do and not do, all the many layers and nuances they must contain. I wanted men to be feminist and progressive and also reflect on their privilege. I wanted men to be equal partners, thoughtful fathers, and dudes who kept their emotional labor demands to them-fucking-selves. But in this phase, this not-looking-for-marriage, not-going-to-have-kids-with-you,

do-not-care-where-this-goes phase, all I needed to know was 6'2".
Firefighter. Lawyer. I texted a photo of him to a friend who shot
back, "I love masculinity."

Suddenly I did, too.

Turned out, I was just this basic. Who cares.

But now he was the one who was too far away. Then again,
now I was the one with a potential date in every Port(land). This
cheered me.

A couple days later I ended up messaging back and forth for
the first time with someone new. Someone handsome. Someone
who dressed so well it made me immediately suspicious. But I
didn't question it. I was training myself to not question every
damn thing.

We switched from OkCupid to WhatsApp and spent nine
straight hours texting. We exchanged stats: siblings (none), parents (two dead, two alive), pets (one dog between us). Only a
month before I had watched my son obsessively check his messages and I couldn't remotely wrap my head around that level of
excitement about anyone or anything. It felt like an alien part of
my past. Then, suddenly, this was who I was. I was checking my
phone every few minutes then every few seconds for a new text, a
new link, did he send a song, what question did he ask? It didn't
help that it was a snow day and I had dumped Baileys in my
coffee at 8:30 a.m., giving myself over to a day I had no control
over anyway.

By the end of the day, I was so horny and overwhelmed I
didn't even understand how I was supposed to go downstairs
and load the dishwasher or perform the multiple bloodless roles
this household required of me. I went to sleep at 10:30 p.m. and
woke up at 1 a.m. and checked my phone. I forced myself back
to sleep, woke again at 5 a.m., checked my phone. There was a
pulse and I could feel it everywhere. I wanted to cry but didn't

know why. I started to theorize that this man was a cyber terrorist or a serial killer. Perhaps both.

And I didn't care.

I had spent the past year berating myself for not seeing every red flag in my marriage. I had forensically excavated where we had gone wrong and wondered why I didn't see it all coming. How could I not see it? Had this not been my own personal Skylab?

I had been relentlessly Monday morning quarterbacking an almost 25-year-long relationship. And the past 36 hours just blew all of that up. Not that I hadn't made genuine progress, not that I hadn't unearthed surprising truths. Not that all of this hadn't been a necessary and sober process. But I was reminded suddenly this was not how love or even basic attraction worked. We don't ever see what's coming. And even if we did, we're just narcissistic enough not to care. Because attraction and the feeling of being in love is narcotic. It is irrational and beautiful, terrifying and overwhelming. And when you try to interrogate it, you worry it'll disappear.

So I gave myself over to all the man-on-a-mountain, man-with-a-fish, man-on-a-mountain-bike, man-in-firefighter-gear, man-scuba-diving, man-doing-man-things-and-looking-manly-doing-them selfies. The last few years made me want to blow my brains out over the toxic mess that was American masculinity. But for now, I just gave in. Clear eyes, full hearts, fuck it. I wasn't here to meet my soul mate. I no longer believed in soul mates at all. *Kinda silly*, I thought to myself, about the entire concept.

I was here for the men.

Phase Five: Lightness

After the initial rush of texting for nine hours and not getting enough sleep, I spent the next day checking my phone roughly two thousand times. There was nothing, and this calmed me. It was an opportunity to remind myself this didn't need to go anywhere. I thought about how this person, this stranger, asked what I wanted from a man and I sat there, stunned. I had spent so many years focusing on what had been missing, what I didn't have, that I hadn't thought enough about what I wanted. I had spent so much time feeling lonely or afraid or sad, I hadn't once stopped to think what would make me happy. Everything I wanted had been in direct response to what I thought I lacked. I had been working from a perceived deficit.

I was overwhelmed by his curiosity and his questions. It had been so long since anyone had been this interested in me and I ate it up with a shovel. It hit me square between the eyes that I could trace everything that had happened over the course of my life, but especially over the past ten years—the writing, all the social media nonsense, an actual book—to this. I had been begging for attention this whole time. I had been begging for it my whole life. I knew this but somehow also didn't realize it. I thought it was "attention" in the abstract, but it was attention in the specific. The people I wanted attention from didn't give it to me, so I asked for it from everyone.

I suddenly felt light. I went about my regular routine, walking the dog, washing the dishes, doing my job, and felt completely above the bullshit. I didn't feel angry or resentful or just old and beaten down. It felt like something had shifted inside of me. It's not that I felt young, that wasn't it. It was that, for the first time, I felt the gravity of my place in my life with joy and without regret.

I didn't care what happened next (although I fantasized about it, constantly). I didn't care if this was where it all ended (although I hoped it didn't). Maybe these ridiculous apps were all I ever needed. Maybe I just needed to be asked.

I waited in my car in front of my kids' school at pickup and turned my music up so loud I was sure it could be heard three cars away, even with my windows up. I didn't care. I was mentally somewhere else. Which, I realized, was what I had wanted all along. I needed to know there was something else out there for me. This, I immediately understood, is why people had affairs.

Phase Six: Horniness

I messaged back and forth with this man almost nonstop for three days. I knew he was wealthy—family money primarily. He had homes in Vermont, Montana, and Virginia. I didn't want to get ahead of myself, but I did anyway. I couldn't imagine launching into a long-term relationship, but I could definitely imagine being rich. Because *finally*. I had been waiting. The relief I felt at just the idea was pornographic. What would I do with all that lack of pressure? In my head I was already living in this stranger's Montana house. I could tell it was big, *so big*. I was there, drinking artisanal coffee from an artisanal mug while wrapped in an even more artisanal robe. I could feel it all.

I imagined, with his background and personal wealth, he was serving in the military through a sense of duty. I was aware of a couple of those types, men who had no financial incentive whatsoever to risk their lives but did so anyway. I admired this.

I began to think about where we might meet between Morrisville and my town when he returned. I chose Waterbury. I imagined we'd meet at a restaurant, probably Prohibition Pig, since wasn't that where everyone met? I began to review outfit options. I began to review hotel options. I began to dwell, often, on how much sex I was about to have. I looked at his picture and thought about him fucking me in all sorts of cliché places like on the kitchen table (gross), in the shower (high stakes), and in his car (high school). I imagined going down on him and imagined his face in between my legs as I reached down to feel his hair between my fingers. I closed my eyes often during my daily routine, sometimes having to place my hand against a wall to steady myself. How was I supposed to live like this? I was genuinely the horniest I had ever been in my entire life.

"Ha ha, ironic, isn't it?!"—The Universe

I was already making arrangements in my head, how I would stay with him over the holiday break. We would meet once, just to confirm the attraction. I considered this housekeeping at this point. Then we would be down there, in his big rich-person house, for a weekend here, an overnight there. I would have to be careful how I worked this with my family but there was no reason to worry about that now. Then he'd be called up again at some point and I'd go back to my life, the one I had just stabilized. But when he was here, I'd be having all the sex a person could possibly have. It was ideal, really.

My mind did occasionally wander to the things that bothered me. I had stuffed these niggling thoughts down initially. Wasn't it just like me to be so judgmental? I got annoyed when he spelled "'cause" as "cos." When he used my first name repeatedly, it just made me think I was in trouble. I felt uncomfortable when he sent me two Enrique Iglesias songs because, well, Enrique Iglesias. But, I told myself, I am too used to being surrounded by cynics and cool people. People who need to be the smartest people in the room with the best taste and the most correct opinions. *Not everyone is like us assholes,* I told myself. *Stop being such a bitch.*

I wondered what it was like to have your only child in boarding school, as he did. I wouldn't even move out of the house I shared with my future ex-husband because I couldn't bear the thought of living apart from my kids until it was either chrono-logically necessary or at least finally felt right to do so. But, as had so often been stated, the rich are different from you and me.

I messaged with him late one night and he said he was up early to prepare a report for a head of state meeting later that day. Being on a dating app as someone doing such sensitive work seemed unwise to me but hey, it wasn't my life.

However.

I continued to be bothered by the fact that his wife, who was a journalist and had died in a plane crash in France in 2015, didn't seem to fit the basic description of anyone on the passenger list I had looked up repeatedly, looking for different and more correct answers. She was not one of the three US vic-tims, based on his general description. Perhaps she was from another country? I certainly wasn't going to ask, because I wasn't a monster.

The morning of my breast ultrasound (a lump was being monitored; this was my life now) he told me he was falling in love with me. Absolutely no thank you. I didn't even respond. But the horniness was still there and had begun to permeate ev-ery aspect of my life. *It wasn't going to be ignored, Dan.*

I went to my appointment and just the act of taking off my top and bra and standing in the glaring light of the dressing room turned me on. This was most definitely a first. I imagined him coming in, drawing the curtain closed. Pressing his weight be-hind me, reaching around and sliding his hand down the front of my pants. I smacked my own face, on both cheeks using both hands, to snap out of it.

I realized as soon as the ultrasound technician asked me to slip my arm out of the sleeve of my gown that we were suddenly playing a very dangerous game. I might inexplicably experience an orgasm in this room. *Ha ha, whoops!*

I was lying down, propped up slightly on my right side by a foam wedge. The room was dark, save for the glow of the screen and an under-cabinet light. She squirted warm ultrasound gel all over my exposed left breast. This was a hair-trigger situation and I could not even believe it. She ran the wand over my breast and clinically measured the lump deep inside. I had never thought less about cancer in my entire life. Between the gel and the motion and my extremely volatile state of arousal, my nipple was all about it. It was standing at attention and ready for some action. It had been waiting so long for this. I was caught between wanting to just let this fucked-up situation play out and wanting to burst out laughing at the absolute absurdity. To look at me in that moment was to see a sexless middle-aged lady at a routine sexless boob exam who underneath it all was very close to getting off.

But then, just like that, it was over. I was pulled back from the brink by an annoying sense of decorum coupled with a slow drip of shame. Get it together, me. But, as had been the case all week, there was still a lightness. I existed in a place above appointments and medical follow-ups, above school forms and working for a living. I was someone who was now capable of having an orgasm in a clinical setting, using only the power of my own perverted mind. *Look at me, everyone. I can do what I want.*

Later that morning I returned to the earlier message, the declaration of love. I did not like it. I did not like it one bit. He followed up with a new photo, one I had not seen yet, of him in uniform. I couldn't get over how hot that was. I couldn't get over how programmed I was to love this. It was like breathing. I stuffed all my doubts down again and stared at the new photo. I took a screenshot of it so I could look at it whenever I wanted.

That afternoon I returned to that photo for maybe the tenth

time. I started to look at the insignia, ribbons, and medals that dotted his uniform. I wanted to know what they meant. I noticed a name tag and tried to zoom in to read it but it was too blurry. I paused for what must've been the twentieth time and wondered how it was possible for him to not show up—anywhere, not even once—in a Google search.

I couldn't really decipher the ribbons all that well. The fact they could be bought on the internet didn't inspire confidence. But I knew he didn't buy them on the internet. I just knew it. He wasn't like that.

Phase Seven: Google

Even so, I started to google a variety of things, because too many details were beginning to bother me. My brain was fighting hard to be heard over my left nipple and my crotch. Finally, a combination of words clicked everything into place, revealing a link that resulted in my face growing hot. It was all right there, right on an Army website, a list of red flags for online romance scams involving the military. It read, in part:

> **Article I. RED FLAGS: some of the words/phrases used by scammers**
> Saying they are on a peacekeeping mission, looking for an honest woman, parents deceased, wife deceased, child being cared for by nanny or other guardian, profess their love almost immediately, refer to you as "my love," "my darling" or any other affectionate term almost immediately, telling you they cannot wait to be with you . . . Finally, they claim to be a U.S. Army Soldier; however, their English and grammar do not match that of someone born and raised in the United States.

He (or whoever) had hit every mark. And I had been his (or whoever's) almost perfect mark. My face was flush with humiliation. At that very moment, my house was coming alive with arrivals at the end of a long work and school day, but I was holed up in the corner of my room wondering *what the fuck now.*

And then I thought, *but I was about to have so much sex* :(

I was more upset about all that future sex evaporating than I was about being at the head of a scam, the rest of the snake having not revealed itself quite yet.

I wanted to nuke every dating app on my phone and then nuke the entire dating app industry personally. I was ashamed of having been fooled. I was embarrassed that I believed any of this could be real. I quickly began to think back through the details of my life that I had shared and was grateful that, given the potential breach, I had shared very little. But still, I had shared some. How else could I connect with other human beings if we weren't exchanging information? Before this experience I could never understand why people would send photos of their breasts or butts or crotches to one another. But I understood it now. I hadn't done it, but I understood the why of it. I understood the immediacy and connection. The exchange felt so private, so personal. Even though I knew—*I actually knew*—it was not. But that was how it felt. And how it felt was everything. This was an experience one hundred percent based on feeling.

He (or whoever) had never asked me for money, not yet. He (or whoever) was methodically building the trust and connection that would make that part easy. The end game was my money. Money for a medical emergency or a flight home, money to cover a paperwork fee or a new cell phone. Suddenly he (or whoever) didn't have access to cash or for some reason the wire he (or whoever) was expecting didn't come, could I help? Didn't

I love him? Then send him money, money, money. Talk about barking up the wrong tree, motherfucker. Bark, bark.

The more it began to sink in, the worse I felt. I didn't feel sad, I felt ashamed. Shame, I continued to be reminded, had been a guiding emotion for much of my life. It had determined my sense of worth and made me mothball my past. It urged me on toward marriage and it had kept me in that marriage. I wanted to take this entire experience to the grave. I didn't want anyone to ever find out about it.

But then I remembered I was a writer so my very next thought was, *or I could tell everyone.*

Hi, everyone.

Phase Eight: Fuckery

Based on how the previous few days had gone, I knew he would be messaging me soon. It was the middle of the night in Africa, you see, where he was on his peacekeeping mission, you absolute dipshit how did I ever fall for this? I was in the process of reverse Google image searching the photos in his profile when I saw his name materialize on my lock screen:

Hello Kimberly
Hope you are having a great day

I was seething. I wanted to block him (or whoever) everywhere we were in contact. But there was also a part of me, the desperate, lonely part of me, that still wanted to believe this wasn't really a scam. But thankfully an even bigger part of me swallowed that other part of me and was like, *come on.*

I let the message sit for a while, I needed to complete my

image search. I found one of the photos populated across multiple Instagram accounts. I couldn't decide who to be angrier at, the scammer or myself. I had felt smug at one point, thinking of how easy this all had been. What were the odds the first man I had a sustained back-and-forth with would be so good-looking and so into me? He didn't look like a model for God's sake, I wasn't a complete idiot (wasn't I, though?). He was *believably* good-looking. Attainably good-looking. I let my mind wander to how fabulous the two of us would look in photos together, how jealous all my boring married friends would be. "Who thinks online dating sucks now, bitch?" I could hear myself saying to them.

Instead there I was with my laptop balanced on one leg as I opened scam-related tab after scam-related tab, and my phone glowed and dimmed with messages. The unnatural glow of a lure in dark, deep waters.

I responded fifteen minutes later:

When will you be back?

Quickly he responded: You mean when will I be coming home?

Me: Yes
Him: I should be home before the end of the year Kimberly. And when am home this time, I just want to get my retirement from the army. I think my son and my woman really needs my time, and that's why I wanna find a woman for myself before getting home this time. With all I have we can live happily and comfortable for the rest of our life

presses fingertips into the space between my eyebrows
Where to even begin. I couldn't get over what a train wreck of

a paragraph this was. I couldn't believe I had tolerated phrases like "my lady" and "my woman." I couldn't begin to fathom the extent to which I had made excuses for the poor grammar and punctuation (would a high-ranking military official really write like this?). I didn't want to know. I couldn't handle the truth, et cetera.

I decided to push on.

> **Me:** Where do you think we should meet that's between your house and Burlington?
> **Him:** I will meet you wherever you want us to meet Kimberly. I'm so eager to meet you babe.

This was all so transparent it was like a windowpane to the face. But, unrelated: I found myself marveling at how I had never been called "babe" before in a relationship and I was surprised to find I didn't hate it. *This has been quite the journey,* I thought, *hasn't it, babe.*

> **Me:** What's your favorite place around there?

I didn't specify where "around there" was.

> **Him:** I don't really have a favorite place, my house is my favorite place Kimberly, so you can just tell me where you will like to meet me

"Uh huh," I said aloud to no one. Now that I knew what I was dealing with it was all so plain. It was all so practiced. I went on to question if his fourteen-year-old son who was away at boarding school would also be back for the holidays. I asked specifically which boarding school he was attending. I was surprised (I was not surprised) to learn it was in Montana and suddenly this was also where he spent most of his time, not Vermont. I asked again for the name of the boarding school, perhaps my friend in Missoula had heard of it? At this he became defensive and asked if I had really never heard of a boarding school in Montana before? I pulled back and said, no, no, it's just that I was much more familiar with the boarding schools in New England (I was not at all familiar with the boarding schools in New England). He calmed down. And changed the subject.

He asked if I was still working. I felt grossed out that I had ever told him anything about my work or my writing and then I had to remind myself he did not give even the slightest fuck about me personally, he was not going to look me up, he was not going to stalk me. He (or whoever) only cared about my money. I changed the subject.

> **Me:** I'd love to get something special to wear when you're back.

I had never said anything like this to a man, that I would dress for him, like a doll. Not that I hadn't dressed specifically for men or in the hopes of luring one of them in, but this was different. Even just pretending made me feel a little sick. But I had to tee up my next question.

He texted back Oh along with eight smiley face emojis surrounded by hearts.

> **Him:** You always sound so loving Kimberly. I'm getting so deeply into you.
> **Me:** Wondering if you could wire me some $ so I could go pick something out?

I sat there grinning, now feeling warm from the inside. I hadn't been wronged romantically in so long I had forgotten what even the most toothless mental games felt like. It was warm, like a hug from a fuzzy monster. It was most enjoyable when the stakes were so low, when I hadn't lost anything more than a bunch of filthy fantasies.

I suffered through a convoluted explanation that fit every element of the scam playbook I had read earlier. How he didn't have access to his money. How his colleagues only survived on the money their wives sent them. And then I was assaulted by this sentence: ". . . since I don't have a woman to do that for me, I survive by whatever is given to me."

I couldn't bring myself to respond immediately, mostly because I genuinely hated this piece of shit. Another message popped up:

Him: I don't know if you understand that
Me: Oh I understand it

This gave him—and I keep using "him" because it's just easier; it could've been a teenage girl, an elderly woman, four chimpanzees in a clown car for all I knew—the perfect window to ask if I was making enough money and how much money *did* I make? I decided to let this question sit overnight. I had an answer ready to go, but why not savor it?

The next morning, as I parked my car and got ready to head into a meeting, a message materialized on my lock screen. I had entered his phone number into my contacts in order to block him, so when the message came up via WhatsApp the recipient read as SCAM.

Scam: Beautiful morning to you over there Kimberly

It was pure poetry. I took a screenshot for posterity. Before I responded I wanted to make sure I was ready to block him on WhatsApp immediately then block him everywhere else as fast as I could. This was my swan song.

Me: Good morning
Scam: How are you doing today Kimberly
Me: Doing so well. How about you? Are you still interested in how much money I make?
Scam: And is that why you stop talking to me yesterday
Me: I was busy, I'm happy to answer your question
Scam: Tell me if you don't mind. I'm just asking to know
Me: I make $$$$GO FUCK YOURSELF$$$$ Go scam someone else

I blocked him. I reported the account. This had all unfolded over a grand total of four days.

Phase Nine: Acceptance

If you're wondering why I haven't used the term *catfishing* or why I seemed somehow unfamiliar with the concept, I have a very simple answer for you. Why would a fifty-one-year-old woman who had been married since 1997—ten years before the iPhone, fifteen years before Tinder—who wasn't actively looking to cheat on her partner, who didn't have a partner who cheated on her, and who wasn't having money suspiciously drained from her bank account give a damn about what catfishing was? How would that term be relevant to my life on any level? I wasn't a stranger to social media or pop culture, but anything even tangentially related to dating, being single, hooking up with strangers, or dating apps didn't register. My attention span for the things that were actually relevant to my life was already finite and failing as it was.

For whatever was lacking in my marriage, a sense of safety and security had not been one of them. I felt comfortable within it and that translated to feeling trusting outside of it. Even though part of me believed people were shit, I was also somehow endlessly gullible.

I could never be a journalist. If I asked a question, I took the first answer available. I don't know why, but I've always been like this. I have almost always trusted what people told me. I believe they are who they say they are. When I was in college I fooled around with a man (boy) who was using a fake accent on me the whole time. I do come by this high-low level of stupidity honestly. But it would be a mistake to underestimate the power of loneliness. Or to underestimate the curative effect of handsomeness upon it.

Handsomeness had been the constant and glowing lure at the ugly mouth of the anglerfish throughout this experience. It took my money from the beginning, I agreed to give it my money. Because I saw handsomeness and I wanted it for myself. I wanted to touch it with my hands and feel its rough face. I wanted to be wrapped in its different arms, run my fingers through its different hair. I wanted to look into eyes that were handsome above a nose that was handsome above a mouth that was the most handsome of all. I never cared if that mouth ever said, "I love you." I would prefer if it didn't. I had given Bumble and Tinder and OkCupid my money, all because of the handsomeness I thought it promised. It was money I handed over at the door, not knowing what this bar was going to be like once I was inside.

Once there, its scarcity made it even more precious, even though I was suspect. Wasn't it so like prey to do that, to pursue something too good to be true? It wasn't like I would ever believe the most handsome man was either a) real or b) interested in me. I often took screenshots of the most handsome men on these apps because where's the crime? The ugliness of the world, my world, my disintegrating life, my boring-ass days full of boring-ass tasks deserved to be countered by men whose facial features really were a salute to genetics, symmetry, and a compliment to their mothers most of all.

I thought I had hedged my bets with an arbitrary range of attractiveness. It would be impossible to articulate what that range was now. To paraphrase the 1964 judgment by Supreme Court Justice Potter Stewart in attempting to define hard-core pornography and obscenity, *I shall not attempt to further define this, but I know it when I see it.* I had not been hit with a man-in-uniform photo up front, that came later. I had not been accosted by what would clearly be understood to be a modeling headshot, that's not what happened. I saw a man in a suit with a sense of style that worked for me. It was the kind of candid photo one would take at a wedding. I had been given just enough information and I had filled in the rest. It was a connect-the-dots with half the lines roughed in and all I had to do was complete the picture.

The lure had worked.

The anglerfish, truly one of the most visually offensive of all aquatic creatures, a creature built from spare nightmares, lures its prey with mesmerizing beauty. The extension that protrudes off its forehead, the one that looks a bit like a fishing pole, evolved from the spine of its dorsal fin. Its origins something prickly, something unforgiving. The glow of the lure comes from the bioluminescent bacteria that inhabit it. This mesmerizing lure looks like one thing but is another thing altogether. It is alive, teeming with creatures the target cannot see. The target will never see them, because the razor teeth and gaping disgusting mouth will have swallowed it whole before it ever gets the chance. But perhaps this target is lucky. Because their mating partners somehow have it worse, as Matt Soniak wrote in "The Horrors of Anglerfish Mating" on the site *Mental Floss*:

> Once the male finds a suitable mate, he bites into her belly and latches on until his body fuses with hers. Their skin joins together, and so do their blood vessels, which allows the male to take all the nutrients he needs from his host/mate's blood. The two fish essentially become one. With his body attached to hers like this, the male doesn't have to trouble himself with things like seeing or swimming or eating like a normal fish. The body parts he doesn't need anymore—eyes, fins, and some internal organs—atrophy, degenerate and wither away, until he's little more than a lump of flesh hanging from the female, taking food from her and providing sperm whenever she's ready to spawn.

Whew, didn't I know it.

I thought about the women who weren't as lucky as I had been, the ones who had actually been scammed. I learned the hard way how easy it could be. I knew what had saved me was an arbitrary constellation of factors. I was in no way looking for a long-term relationship. That was the dead last thing I was looking for. I was not religious—he had specifically asked if I was Christian, if I believed in God. I thought about how manipulative and genuinely evil that question had been. Although I was emotionally and sexually lonely, I lived in a house with other people I loved and could talk to and hug. I had affectionate and physical touch available to me. I had connection. I had a network of intimate friends I trusted, I had work that engaged me, creative pursuits that fulfilled me. For years I had focused on what I didn't have, but in this upside-down, opposite-world equation, I had more than I had realized.

All of this had protected me, in part, from this cynical targeting. These predators were handpicking victims by fiddling with the levers of their humanity—faith, loneliness, insecurity, hunger for emotional connection, hunger for physical connection, hunger to be understood and loved, the desire for someone to just ask them a simple question about what they wanted. From the beginning, long before the prey would be eviscerated by the razor teeth and the gaping wet and dark mouth, they had been constructing a way to never be found out. They had sealed it all with shame, an emotional jail of silence. They would make anyone feel humiliated for wanting what would make them feel whole.

I had demonstrated stalking tendencies in my twenties, pre-Google, pre–social media. Finally, all these years later, it had paid off and inoculated me. I knew people couldn't be ghosts in the digital world. I knew they would come up in property records or court records, a LinkedIn page or Facebook. We were all leaving breadcrumbs across the internet, it was impossible not to. And sometimes, even though we were guilty of nothing more than existing, our images could be stolen and regurgitated onto some poor, lonely person. That poor, lonely person could be sitting right next to you at the dinner table, waiting in the car in front of you at school pickup, praying alongside you at church, sitting with you at book club.

That poor, lonely person could be me.

I decided this had been a test. And I had passed.

I looked through our messaging history and I hadn't said anything negative about Jon other than the simple fact our marriage no longer worked and was ending. I referred to him as kind, a talented carpenter, a good person. This slow undoing of our marriage, of building a friendship to outlast it, had just been stress tested. I was not loyal to him in the intimate sense (not that I owed him that)—make no mistake, I was one hundred percent ready to travel regularly for no strings attached sex—but I was loyal to him in the only ways that mattered now. I felt protective. I was not going to talk shit about him. I would not participate in a house unnecessarily divided more than it already was. Where would that get me?

I went downstairs for dinner and was overwhelmed by the normalcy I saw all around me. I felt like I had just reentered the atmosphere and smashed back down onto the surface of my own life. I knew this life. These were real people I could see, real people I loved, real people I understood even when I didn't understand them at all. No one here was going to refer to me as "my woman." If anyone here was lying to me, they were telling me the lies that kept polite society humming along.

Everyone lies.

Everyone, at some point, is lying to themselves most of all.

Phase Ten: Reentry

I wasn't ready to leave this ludicrous experiment behind. What did I expect? That it would work out? What a joke. But I couldn't deny, even given everything that had happened, I had still re-tained that lightness. I had tapped into an alternate life, as fleet-ing and false as it was, and it had set me free. I ran into friends I had held unspoken grudges against and felt no anger. Some-where along the way, in the midst of this fucked-up experience, I had been changed. To be mad at everyone where I lived was to accept this small life was going to be my life forever. It was to re-sent the people who populated it, cursing them just for existing, for staying married, for having annoying small town questions (normal human questions) about my annoying small town life.

But now? Now I knew there would be another life out there for me. I didn't know what it was yet or what it looked like, but I knew it was there. I could feel it. Less than 24 hours later I was scanning and swiping again, feeling three weeks older and debatably wiser.

I was back to the deep, dark waters.

I was back, looking for the glow.

Things People Say When You Get Divorced That They Really Should Say When You Get Engaged

"Oh, I'm so sorry!"

"Couldn't you just have an affair instead?"

"Want to get drunk?"

"Did you guys try therapy?"

"Wow, what the hell happened??"

"Which stage of grief are you in?"

"Well, you *have* been acting strange."

"I know exactly one other person going through this, you should date them."

"I think you're making a mistake."

"Maybe you should try a different therapist?"

"We already secretly did this but are too ashamed to tell anyone."

"What did *he* do?"

"What did *you* do?"

"You should get on Tinder."

"Are you sure this is for the best?"

"Yeah, I don't get it."

"That's really sad :(:(:("

"Maybe you should pray about it."

"How are you?" (whispers) *"No how are you, really?"*

"Are you having some sort of crisis?"

"This feels so sudden. Are you sure?"

"Can't you just buy a sports car instead?"

"Well, just goes to show this could really happen to anyone."

"But you seemed so happy."

"Therapy."

Nuts and Bolts

We thought it was temporary, so we didn't think to make rules.

I still did the laundry and folded the clothes because it's the one thing I've done throughout my life that gives me a sense of mindless, tangible completion. He continued to make most of the meals, a shift in labor that happened after I tearfully exploded for what felt like the hundredth time, trying to explain that the person who had the palate of a five-year-old, hated cooking, and would never learn how because there were other things I wanted to do with my life, *was not the person who should be cooking for our children.* Especially given he was *an excellent cook.*

I stopped inserting myself into, caring about, or facilitating his communication with his family. In general I took myself out of the role of Head of Communications as well as Chief Birthday Present Buyer and Happy Anniversary Caller and Human Walking Reminder Lady and it felt as good as it sounds.

We went to school events, parties, and other gatherings together. We saw our friends separately, too, but we had always done that. We had never been a couple nor a family who always did everything all together all the time, so in that respect not much changed.

I stopped going camping. I didn't hate camping, actually. But I didn't love it enough to keep going when opting out and having a weekend to myself was an option. One of our closest friends, my design partner, Dabbs, started going in my place. Whenever they're all on camping trips together I think about how other campers probably assume they're a double dad family or, to my endless delight, a Double Dabbs family.

The summer after we announced our divorce I glanced down at his iPad on the kitchen counter when an email came up on his lock screen. He was at work. The email was from a woman I didn't know. The first few lines that were visible said that, yes, she actually might take that golf class with him and my son and I was like *what the fuck is this shit.* I thought I didn't care what he did and I would be happy for him when he moved on, because I was now an Evolved Person. Instead I was shocked at how flashy and visceral my jealousy was. He could move on after I moved on! I'd be happy for him after I was happy for myself first! We texted back and forth in a delicate flurry. He said she was just a friend and of course he would've told me if anything was going on. We agreed to this as our first rule. Anything happens, you go on a date, anything along those lines, there needs to be a conversation. We agreed that that'd probably be the beginning of the end of this little arrangement (and this is still our assumption).

A couple months later, he was cleaning up after having ripped up all the carpet in my new bedroom. It was a surprise birthday present for me, getting the floor prepped and ready to paint. I was sitting on the floor, scrolling through my phone as it charged, and realized that per our agreement I should tell him I had joined Tinder that afternoon. So I did. And he said, "okay," and that was the entirety of his reaction. I never ended up going on a single real date, so I never told him anything that happened while I was on any dating apps. The whole experience was so weird and theoretical and stupid. But when he read this book, one of the things he was most upset by was my dating app story. He said, "We had agreed we would tell each other if we were dating anyone," and I was like, "I was almost scammed ??? by a con man/person ??? and that is not dating ???" We agreed to disagree. ¯_(ツ)_/¯

I still pay all the bills from our joint account and we still pool the majority of our money. We've always had separate personal checking accounts and we separated our credit cards the year before we agreed to divorce. I have kept him (and our children) as a beneficiary on all my accounts, policies, and benefits. I have no intention of leaving him high and dry should anything happen to me. That is not how our marriage worked. He allowed me to work as hard as I could and I encouraged him to pursue a job that would make him happy no matter how much it paid, either cooking or carpentry, and I will never forget any of those deliberate choices.

We ask about each other's days and talk about them more now than we did before. Sometimes all four of us will watch a show or a movie after dinner but more often than not we are scattered to our various shows, work, books, games, and FaceTimes with friends. We are a house of four separate adults, two young, two oldish, and there is a communal, roommate-ish feeling to so much of our lives now. On the one hand I'm grateful we're independent people, each with room to roam inside our own home. But I'd be lying if I didn't say I sometimes worry about how this mirrors my own teenage years, especially when we each grab dinner and retreat to our own corners.

I could go on, but the list would be tedious and the takeaway would be the same—some things stayed the same, some things we couldn't plan for, and some things we do completely differently.

Our approach reminds me a little of a realization I had the day after getting laid off from a job that had become a cornerstone of my identity. I had worked so hard, I had given my life over to it, I had left my small children during dinners and weekends because of that job. But what struck me the morning after I was laid off was this singular thought: *Maybe I could just do what I'm good at now instead of everything I was made to feel bad about.*

Our current arrangement, our prelude to a divorce, is like that. We are just doing what we are good at and not doing the things we were bad at (mostly). It is a relief to be free of the should-we-get-a-divorce talks. It is a relief to be free of the darkness and uncertainty that loomed over me for so many years. It is a relief to no longer feel bad for not being in love with someone or them not being in love with me because it happens! It is a relief to be out in the open and transparent about how we are living even if everyone around us finds it utterly weird and confusing. I just don't give a fuck about that.

It feels like the glamorous future.

Creating Our Grief

We all have our types. Not just in partners but in articles. There are subjects we're drawn to and headlines we can't resist, even when we know we're being manipulated. Sometimes especially then.

My drug of choice used to be working mothers, breastfeeding, and daycare: good or bad? Also women who earn more than their partners, women who manage more than their partners, and women who are ready to absolutely lose their shit permanently. Then my interests shifted to include the history of marriage and just about anything about divorce except self-help (ha). Also: feminism, rage (redundant?), ageism, and, perhaps not surprisingly, living alone on an island.

But if we're talking evergreen content, it would be tough to beat the passage of time. Melancholy over how regular life unfolds. The struggle to recognize that no matter how much we want to, we can never go back. We can't crawl back into a memory. We can no longer touch the face of a person now long gone. We will never again be the younger version of ourselves. We must keep moving forward, toward the unknowable horizon. Children grow up, people change—why do you think "Landslide" has all those lyrics?

Becoming a mother only intensified my desire to dig into all of this, to force it between my fingers like Play-Doh and watch it squish through. Surely there has to be something new here. Or if not new, at least more to my liking. Surely there must be better answers by now.

Children are the undeniable markers of time. We can see not only year-to-year but sometimes day-to-day that time will swallow us all whole. We wonder if we are making the most of it now. We wonder what we would do differently then. We often think the time for action is in the future, when we will surely get it right. And then we arrive at the allotted time realizing we have done so little of what we had set out to do. We were so sure we would. But the years had somehow grown shorter, they shot by faster, and now we feel haunted by everything we left undone.

I regret to inform you I have always been this way. Even when I was in high school I was obsessed with the passage of time. Because of my intense diary habit, sometimes writing in two or three different journals simultaneously and separated by subject matter, I'd call up my best friend, Aimee, and say things like, "A year ago today we were at your house wrapping Christmas presents together. It was three days after we bought that sad Charlie Brown Christmas tree at that weird lot, remember?" which would inevitably lead to the question, "How do you know that?" or maybe the implied question was "What is wrong with you? Who looks back in high school?"

I had written it all down. These small mundane moments, quotes drawn from song lyrics, insipid entries wholly focused on boys who were morons, all the important work of being my specific version of a teenage girl. I had been alive for less than twenty years and was already fluent in nostalgia, constantly revisiting the past, longing for what had already happened. I wonder now if that obsession was how my anxiety first began to express itself. The past was comforting. I already knew what had happened. The future? The unexpected? Not very cool. No surprises? Extremely cool. Also, one of my favorite Radiohead songs.

I couldn't have anticipated one day my personal nostalgia obsession would scale up into a nostalgia industrial complex. TWO YEARS AGO TODAY, FIVE YEARS AGO TODAY, Facebook, Instagram, Google pics. Even Snapfish (Snapfish! Remember Snapfish?) serves me regular reminders of what was going on back when I was using Snapfish. And I was using Snapfish when my kids were infants and then toddlers, before the iPhone was invented, before Facebook rolled out to the public, and before Instagram existed. That means every album contained the early days of my family, my young children, a marriage far in the background but matter-of-factly there like a fieldstone foundation. My curly-haired, bright-eyed girl; my beautiful boy. We were a family. Everything would flow from that point, a headwater.

I couldn't have anticipated when I was a teenager that my concept of life in constant review would become so popular, although I could've told anyone who cared how manipulative and deceptive it would be. "Look at what you did, look at how much better you had it, look at what you didn't pay attention to at all, look at these babies, look at these moments—they are gone forever. Here, look again. Does it hurt yet? Are you crying? Do you even know what you're crying about? Don't you remember some of these moments were tangled up with frustration, exhaustion, messes, and disappointment? Don't you remember you were struggling, truly struggling, during some of these theoretical highlights? Do you remember how you desperately wanted things to start getting easier which, by default, meant you were wishing the time away? Do you miss it now? Do you wish you had it back? Hey, isn't life dumb?"

Needless to say, if you've written for a major publication about these sorts of things, I have probably read it. If you examine your everyday sadnesses and invite others to do the same this is what I have to say to you—*Give me that sweet, sweet stuff. Yes, right there, yes, just like that.*

I will often skim these pieces first, because that's how reading works now, pre-reading to determine if reading-reading is worth it. Even when I commit, I can't help but think, *surely with us all rapidly spinning toward the end of The Great American Experiment does it make sense to be writing about something so . . . regular life?* This is, no doubt, the inherent bias I've both learned and experienced when it comes to women writing about their lives. As if centuries of men haven't been packing shelves with microscopic examinations of their every passing thought and fart, every inaccurately sketched breast glimpsed through a gap in a blouse, or cringingly described penis's slightest reactions to a breeze.

But I've always been a melancholy soul, drawn to lowercase sadness. When *A Charlie Brown Christmas* is your favorite holiday special, that tells you something about who you are. It tells you that you enjoy the adrenaline of low-key, low-stakes grief. The type of grief you feel from simply being alive. I rarely place my one small life in the context of a big and tragic world. I consistently dismiss my relentless good fortune. I constantly look back, noticing how good things were then and now look. Look what I had made of it. Look what I had lost. Look at these mistakes, all of them, scattered at my feet. What a loss. What a loser. Only to look back a few years from now and reflect on how good I had had it. Those were the days.

And so, naturally, I live for these sad regular-life pieces. They're the mature upgrade to my high school diary entries. If I have a strong reaction to an article along these lines, I'm immediately drawn to the comments. I'm curious: Will they confirm how I'm feeling or what I thought as I read it? Am I experiencing the correct emotions? Or will the comments be awash in pearl-clutching outrage? Will there be compliments, a connection made? Or will they just be the stinky hellmouth of the non-thinking universe, as they so often are? Parenting pieces in particular, especially those written by women, tend to incite three main reactions: 1) You shouldn't have children and you shouldn't be a mother, how dare you, 2) Wow, must be nice to spend all your day having emotions about things! and 3) This is me, I get this, I get you, thank you.

When mothers write about mothering, it is especially fraught when men insert themselves into the conversation. I always brace myself when I see a man's name attached to a comment, for surely he will be insufferable and off base, insulting and patronizing. Also, no one was *fucking asking him*. Can't we just have one corner of the internet to ourselves already?

And then it happened. I came upon one particularly melancholy piece about children growing up and moving on to their adult lives. I scrolled right on over to the comments. Parenting commenters love to tell other parents to get their shit together. They love to eye roll and feel superior when anyone dares to publicly express an experience. And how dare the writer take that experience and turn it over in their hands, examining it? Stop being such a baby and worry about real things! Even when the piece itself is saying, "I know I should stop being such a baby and worry about real things!" It's never good enough, which at least is a fitting takeaway for the subject of motherhood.

But on this piece I noticed a comment from a man named Ed. I was afraid of what Ed might say. Partly because I identified with the writer of this piece, she was where I'd be in just a few short years. But also because Ed was a man who lived in Wisconsin. Although I had also lived in Wisconsin and knew it to be a nice place with nice people, I was now a coastal elite who drank lattes while listening to NPR in my Volvo and therefore it was in my nature to feel suspicious of the Midwest and all of its citizens.

This is what Ed from Wisconsin had to say, in part:

We create our grief by expecting life to be different than it is.

What.

I narrowed my eyes and stared at that one line. How dare Ed from Wisconsin electrify me like this? How dare the comments section on a parenting piece punch me in the chest and be relevant not only to my present interests but my future ones as well? How dare one single comment from a man I did not know so drastically shift my perspective? *Hi, I'm Ed. Hold onto your skull because I'm about to blow your mind.* *tips hat*

It reminded me of a lunch I had had with another man, a friend, a few months before. I felt completely unhinged and I felt bad about that unhinged feeling. Feeling unhinged at fifty is quite different than feeling unhinged at, say, twenty-eight. At twenty-eight you can arrogantly assume you have loads of runway left. Unhinged is even a bit adorable when you're that age, like you're the lead character in your own rom-com. If you're fifty and unhinged, your movie is going to be a drama and it will not be a good one.

Anyway, we weren't even close. I saw him maybe twice a year. But even with acquaintances I had lost all ability or interest in pretending life was peachy. Acting that way is something of a community service, alleviating the pressure on others to care. But I was too wrapped up in how I felt to worry about how I made other people feel anymore.

Here is one of the best things about men: They typically won't vibe you out the way a woman will. Most of them don't know how. You're on different teams, you just are. They're not judging you in about thirteen different categories the way another woman might. Men do not try to give you eating disorders like other women do. Don't get me wrong, men are to blame for them *of course*, the patriarchy and so on and so forth but *I don't have time to get into that right now.*

My point being, I genuinely like men even if men are not completely convinced of this. And one of the reasons is that sometimes—and, believe me, it pains me to say this—men are just better at bypassing the emotion inherent in a situation, coolly assessing it, then hitting you with a nine-word insight, max.

I had gone on and on over lunch about how afraid I was, without using that exact word. I theoretically knew why I felt that way on a rational level (I was getting a divorce!) and on an emotional level (I was getting a divorce!), but I was also so in the weeds that I had no perspective whatsoever. It was my life, it's not like I could examine it from a distance. All the turmoil I had been feeling was leading to both panic and paralysis. I felt somehow simultaneously unmoored and trapped, truly the Chinese finger puzzle of emotions.

He listened. He nodded. He drank his soda and was probably chewing on an ice cube when he dropped in with, "Well nothing in your life is stable. That's why."

Ha ha are you shitting me? As I drove away from our lunch I ran down the full list instead of the immediate and abbreviated one. I was financially unstable, emotionally unstable, transitioning out of the most important relationship of my life, and every day my children separated just a little bit more from me. I no longer wanted to live where we lived but I couldn't leave. Every step I wanted to take, in absolutely any and every direction, was a step on shaky ground.

Of course.

Of course this is why I felt the way I did.

Of course.

We create our grief by expecting life to be different than it is.

When I got married and when I had children I thought I was done searching for happiness. I had it all right here, right in front of me. I thought it would be a permanent state of being. I thought I was done feeling unsettled. I thought my children would be children forever. I didn't rationally believe this, of course, but when children are children you can't wrap your head around them ever being adults and leaving even though this is something you yourself once did. You have experience in this area.

I expected life to be easy and ordered, because how could anything be worse than the desperation and loneliness I felt when I was in my twenties and single? Or was I even remembering that correctly? Or was it just that everyone around me was getting married and I didn't want to be left behind? Sometimes you're just going on dates and then everyone you know is getting married and you go to those weddings and, hey, that looks like fun and suddenly you've got your own lifelong commitment that maybe you wouldn't have made had the timing been different.

I thought marriage meant we were set, as the vows go, for life. I thought it just happened. I thought it needed little to no work, like a cactus. I thought I would be taking one if not two vacations a year, nothing luxurious, just certain. I thought we would always take beautiful pictures together at magic hour. I thought we would look at them and say to each other, "Look at her. Look at him. Look at our family. Look at how we've got it all figured out."

Incredibly for a cynic, I somehow believed life was an endless unfolding of happiness, achievement, and security. I thought he would always love me. I thought I would always love him. What was the point of thinking otherwise? I thought we would have more over time. Less was never even on the menu.

Minus true grief—the wrenching work of mourning—my daily grief is fully inside me and within my control. I conjure it into being with my expectations. I feed it and let it course through my veins. I say I don't want to feel this way, but sometimes I do. It makes me feel *something*.

What would happen if I walked away from my expectations? What if I stopped operating from the past? What if I refused to compare myself to my former self, my younger self? What if I stopped comparing my teenage children to their toddler selves, the end of my marriage now to the beginning of my marriage then? What if I started afresh, every morning, right where I stood? What if I accepted the hand I'd been dealt? What if I accepted I had done much of that dealing myself?

What if, as women, we didn't do what society keeps pushing us to do—to apologize for the offense of continuing to live? What if we refused to stand naked in the mirror for the sole purpose of mourning and hating ourselves?

What if I looked at my spotty arms and instead of seeing all the mistakes—the baby oil applied in the sun, the tricep dips left undone—I instead saw those arms and those spots were answers to this equation:

How many beach days + how much walking on my lunch hour in the city wearing short sleeves on the first warm days of spring + how many road trips with my arm out the open window, swooping up and down with the wind + how many babies carried + look at all this holding + look at me still living.

What if I looked at my children and saw them not as traitors for growing up and away from me, becoming somehow simultaneously more and less known to me, but instead the people they are right in this very moment? People who, like me, like Jon, are struggling to figure it all out. People who genuinely need empathy and affection, no matter how prickly or assured they may sometimes seem. They're already looking ahead and around and behind them. What if I showed them this, right here, is where their lives start? Every day, right in this very spot.

What if we *all* looked at our marriages not as they were in those early years and instead focused on what that marriage was or was not giving us, right now? Is it enough? Are we doing enough, individually, to make it work? Do we even care? Are we still in love? What does that mean, in both practical and fanciful terms? How happy is happy enough? Are we okay wanting more? Feeling emotionally greedy? What if we gave our marriages a daily performance review instead of finding ourselves twenty years later wondering what the fuck happened? Or what if we just accepted relationships run their course and stop viewing that as a moral failing? Relationships in every other part of our lives dissolve and disappear yet we rarely imbue those completed relationships with such a deep sense of failure and shame.

What if we gave up on the idea of forever? For everything? What if we worried less about the people who were at our wedding and what they thought? In fact, what if we said to ourselves *I don't care what other people think of me at all. I'm done.* What if we just stopped performing for other people, period? No more sing-songy voices as you talk to your six-year-old in front of other parents. No more cleaning the house from top to bottom just because a certain judgmental acquaintance *who you don't even like* is going to breeze over for all of thirty seconds to drop off a book or a borrowed sled or whatever the fuck. No more wasting energy trying to control the uncontrollable: Other people. Time.

Anxiety introduces us to a sinister fill-in-the-blank, "But what if _____" and we endlessly fill it with worst-case scenarios. What if I'm alone forever, what if I get sick and no one cares, what if someone I love dies, what if no one ever loves me again, what if everyone's disappointed in me, what if I end up without a penny to my name, what if I did absolutely everything wrong? *But what if* we asked ourselves instead, "But what if it all turns out okay?"

What if I stopped expecting life to be different than it is?

This is me, today. I am going to accept this is where I am. That the past is done. The future is unknown and never guaranteed. I am going to feel grateful for what I have and forgive myself for my mistakes. I am going to accept I've probably made fewer of them than I think. I am going to move forward, without regret. I am going to tell the hater in me who looks in the mirror and tells me how old I look, what a piece of shit I am, and how dare I even dress up and go out like I deserve happiness—I am going to tell that voice to zip it, lock it, put it in its motherfucking pocket.

I am done creating my grief.

I am going to love this life.

I am going to love me, today.

When Sally Divorced Harry

FADE IN:
INT. DINER—MORNING
CARD: MANHATTAN, 2007

HARRY BURNS, now 59, and SALLY ALBRIGHT, now 46, are seated in a booth, looking over the breakfast menu. They seem tense. A WAITRESS comes over and pours coffee without asking.

> **WAITRESS**
> Ready to order?

> **HARRY**
> Coffee. Well, apparently. And I'll take the Lumberjack Special.

> **SALLY** (*snorts*)

> **HARRY**
> Is there a problem with me ordering the Lumberjack Special?

SALLY

Harry, I am perfectly fine with you ordering the Lumberjack Special. [to the waitress] Yes, I'll have the French toast, but I would like it made with sourdough not white. I'll have whipped cream but only if it's fresh and not from a can. I'd like strawberries also only if they're fresh but if not then I don't want any. And I'd like butter and syrup but on the side.

HARRY

Can't you order like a normal person, just once? Just one time could you have a meal that doesn't scream, *hey everyone I'm a cross between a five-year-old and the oldest person alive?*

SALLY

Harry, I've always ordered like this. You know I've always ordered like this. You used to love it.

HARRY

Well turns out I hate it.

SALLY

You know what I hate, Harry? You pretending to be twenty-six when we met even though you were actually forty-one.

HARRY

Get outta here. You were twenty-eight, pretending to be twenty!

SALLY

I love how an eight-year age difference for me is somehow a more serious crime than a fifteen-year age difference for you. Give me a break.

HARRY

Oh there are some things I'd like to break. You know what I'd like to break?

SALLY

No, Harry, what?

HARRY

I'd like to break this salt and pepper shaker set because does anyone love the idea of two pigs shedding salt and pepper all over their food? I'd like to break this ridiculous ashtray because no one even smokes anymore! But most of all I'd like to break this stupid wedding ring with its stupid FOREVER inscription because how stupid can two people really be?

SALLY

Once again I'd like to remind you you don't need to express every feeling you have every moment you have them.

HARRY

How can you be so calm? How is it possible that I, a person who can order breakfast without a legally binding contract, *am the irrational one?*

SALLY
I don't know, Harry. I don't know anymore.

HARRY *(whispers)*
What do you want, Sally?

SALLY
I don't know, Harry, why don't you flip to the
last page of this book and tell me how it ends.

HARRY
You were the one who wanted this. *You* wanted
marriage more than anything. It's all you
thought about, it's practically all we ever talked
about. We ended up sleeping together because
your stupid ex Joe got stupidly engaged like the
stupid Ken doll that he was!

SALLY
Excuse me? Are you really trying to blame me
for the first time we had sex? [starting to yell]
I'm sorry, Harry, I hadn't realized you fucked
me completely against your will!

Realizing they're causing a scene SALLY leans in closer and
lowers her voice.

SALLY *(CONT'D)*
And what about you? You wanted this, too.
You're the one who rushed to that New Year's
Eve party and professed your love for me in

front of everyone! And you'd already been
married! Shouldn't you have known better?!

HARRY pauses and softens. HARRY reaches his hand across
the table and places it on SALLY'S hand.

HARRY
Are you finished?

SALLY
Yes.

SALLY withdraws her hand and puts it in her lap.

HARRY
Can I say something?

SALLY
Yes.

HARRY
I'm sorry. I just . . . I just miss us.

SALLY
You miss the idea of us.

HARRY
No I miss the whole us.

SALLY
The whole us was a very long time ago, Harry.

FADE IN:
DOCUMENTARY FOOTAGE

of a YOUNG COUPLE, a WOMAN and a MAN, sitting together on a loveseat. They're smiling and at ease with one another. She's wearing an engagement ring. They speak directly to the CAMERA.

> JILL *(admiring her ring)*
> I don't know, it just felt right. Didn't it feel right?

> JAMES *(squeezes her hand, looks at her lovingly)*
> Yeah, it really did.

> JILL
> What else do you need to know as long as you're in love?

FADE OUT.

FADE IN:
EXT. FUNERAL HOME—DAY
CARD: SEVEN YEARS LATER

SALLY exits the funeral home and opens her purse looking for a fresh Kleenex. HARRY navigates through the crowd and catches up to her.

> HARRY
> Hey. I thought I saw you in there.

SALLY (*blows her nose loudly*)
Remember when you thought dwelling on
death made you seem edgy?

HARRY
Well it was more fun when it wasn't actually
happening to people I know.

SALLY (*begins to cry again*)
I can't believe Marie's gone. Of course I
knew she'd be gone and we'll all be gone
but I thought she'd be gone, you know,
some . . . day.

HARRY
And Jess.

SALLY
And Jess, too. I know, I heard. I'm sorry.

HARRY
Yeah.

SALLY
I still can't believe he left her. Who was *he* to
leave *her*?

HARRY
He's dead, Sally. That's who.

SALLY
Right. I know, I'm sorry. I just—

HARRY

He should've never gotten rid of that wagon
wheel coffee table.

SALLY

Harry.

HARRY

What? He shouldn't have. I told him. Don't
get me wrong that thing was hideous, but
still, I warned him. Anyway, want to grab a
sandwich?

SALLY

How can you eat right now?

HARRY

We were married for twenty years, how can you
ever be surprised by me eating?

SALLY

Fine.

FADE IN:
DOCUMENTARY FOOTAGE

of a different YOUNG COUPLE, a MAN and a WOMAN,
sitting together on the same loveseat. They're both wearing
wedding rings. She is chatty and bubbly, he is more reserved
and looks direct to CAMERA the entire time.

CHARLOTTE

All our friends were getting married, it felt like
we were going to a wedding every weekend!

MICHAEL

It sure . . . did.

CHARLOTTE

And it was just kind of like, what are we waiting
for? It's not like we're getting any younger!

MICHAEL

[long pause] We are . . . not.

FADE OUT.

FADE IN:
EXT. CENTRAL PARK—FALL AFTERNOON
CARD: FOUR YEARS LATER

HARRY is walking and holding hands with a woman who is
clearly younger than him. SALLY is coming toward them from
the opposite direction, walking a sleek cream-colored Afghan
Hound. They notice each other at the same time.

SALLY

Hi, Harry.

HARRY

Sally, it's been a while.

SALLY *(looking brightly at the woman then
back to Harry)*

It sure has.

HARRY

Sorry—Sally this is Jessica. Jessica, Sally. Sally
and I were—

SALLY *(extending her hand)*

—married.

JESSICA

Nice to meet you. Harry talks about you all the
time.

SALLY

Does he really?

JESSICA

Oh yeah, he says you like to order—

HARRY

Alright, alright, enough of that. [kneels down
to talk to the dog] Who's this handsome guy
right here? Did you name him Joe? They have
the same hair.

SALLY

Very funny. His name is Sheldon.

HARRY *(smiling)*

You didn't.

SALLY

I most certainly did. [to Jessica] Did Harry tell
you his real age?

HARRY

Seventy-two, yes. But the women of Manhattan
thank you for your vigilance. Well, we should
be on our way. It was really nice to see you.

SALLY

You too, Harry. [pauses] Jessica.

HARRY and JESSICA walk away.

SALLY *(to the dog)*

You have much better hair than Joe. Especially
now that he doesn't have any.

FADE IN:
DOCUMENTARY FOOTAGE

of HARRY and SALLY, each sitting on a chair in the same style
of the loveseat seen previously. Their chairs are placed side by
side. They speak directly to the CAMERA.

SALLY

He didn't think a man could be friends with a
woman without wanting to have sex with her.

HARRY

Well the sex part did get in the way.

SALLY

Until it didn't.

HARRY

Until it didn't.

SALLY

I was so afraid of turning 40.

HARRY

Until you did.

SALLY

Until I did.

HARRY

I think we put too much emphasis on New
Year's Eve.

SALLY

Tell me about it.

HARRY

And too little maybe on other things.

SALLY

A lot of other things. But we've known each
other practically our whole lives at this point.

HARRY

And now look at us.

They look at each other and smile. SALLY reaches for HARRY'S hand and gives it a squeeze.

SALLY
Friends.

HARRY puts his arm around the back of her chair.

HARRY
Really good friends.

SALLY
It's how this story ends.

FADE OUT.

Epilogue: Adult Swim

What if we're not better after all this?

What if we haven't learned a damn thing?

What if this was all for nothing?

I thought I understood the path Jon and I were on, loosely anyway. I thought I understood how the phases might work. One of us would date someone, then the other would date someone. We would finally unravel this high-minded experiment and go about breaking apart our household like people who just did things the normal wrenching way for a change. Band-Aid off, finally.

As the months passed, I began to wonder if this whole thing hadn't been a mistake. Not the divorce but our "divorce." I worried by drawing it out to make the break feel less traumatic for our kids (and let's face it, easier on us), we had just extended the pain and filled their lives with uncertainty for longer than necessary. After all, we were still going on vacation together, throwing parties together, going to school events together. What had really changed?

My daughter broke down several times, wondering if a fairly mundane yet explosive disagreement over screen time or chores was the last straw and one of us would move out. I was reminded often your intentions when raising kids hardly matter, it all boiled down to which mirror they choose to hold up to you at any given point. Is it the one with the accurate reflection or was it that fun house one? I'm sorry, no one ordered these distortions, please take them back to the carnival where you got them.

But that path, and every mirror available to us, ceased to fit within a system we understood. Because no matter what I was expecting from marriage or divorce or our seemingly never-ending separation, I'll tell you one thing, I sure as shit wasn't expecting a global pandemic.

In late January and again in late February, I had flown cross-country for work, returning from Bay Area airports where TSA agents wore masks even though we had all been told not to. On my very last flight back to Vermont I scarfed down a Toblerone, an airport-based habit I had picked up twenty years earlier when I would buy a Toblerone multipack at Schiphol in Amsterdam and "accidentally" finish it by the time I arrived back in the States. The chocolate had melted all across my fingertips and as I instinctively went to lick them I thought, you know what, maybe I shouldn't.

I had returned home just in time for my kids' February school break and spent almost the entire time complaining. I couldn't concentrate on work and hated being forced to stop what I was doing to make my kids lunch, but if I didn't one of them just wouldn't eat and the other would graze all day long. It felt like making lunch for them was somehow both the least and the most I could do. I complained about not being able to think clearly when everyone was home, when I had to keep other people's needs and schedules in my head. I couldn't wait until things got back to normal! That school break—what we used to adorably refer to as the "long break"—had been eleven days long. There are times when it's a mercy not to know what's coming.

Then we were into March, the worst month in Vermont, no matter the year. On Friday the 13th—of course—my kids' teachers told them to bring everything home with them, just in case schools closed. On the 15th, our governor ordered schools to close no later than Wednesday, March 18th. We had told our kids Monday and Tuesday were it, the last two days they'd be in school for a while. We knew the closure wasn't likely to last just two and a half weeks as originally announced, but we certainly didn't expect that only nine days later schools would be shut down to in-person instruction for the remainder of the year. We certainly didn't know how quickly and permanently all our lives were about to crash down and fold in on themselves.

That Monday morning, March 16th, the last normal Monday morning, we were running through a morning routine we'd been through hundreds, thousands, of times. My son not brushing his teeth until I asked if he had and my daughter running around the house packing up her belongings and looking for her hairbrush. I tried to decide whether I should walk the dog before the bus came or after, not that two teenagers needed me there anyway. But I liked to be there to watch through the window as the bus drove by. It was one of the many things I appreciated about our school system and neighborhood after having spent years driving my kids to and from daycare and every one of their previous schools.

I happened to walk through the living room just as the earlier bus, the elementary school bus, that big yellow metal caterpillar, slipped by our picture window. Empty. It was a ghost bus with only a driver who paused tentatively at each stop then mournfully moved on. No little faces in the windows, no kids turned this way and that chatting with one another. No child pressing their forehead to the window, looking out, willing themselves to be anywhere else. Maybe missing their mom or their dog. None of that.

Ten minutes before their bus would arrive I wanted to tell them they couldn't go. But I didn't. I could already feel the emotional architecture of school beginning to collapse. Instead I said, "I know I told you you could go on Tuesday, too. But I think today is it."

I have a photo of the last bus they took, the middle school and high school bus, as it slid past our window. I can see the silhouette of my son making his way down the aisle of the bus, lugging his cumbersome baritone sax case. And I can see my daughter's face clearly in the window. Normally she'd wave quickly, if at all, and jump right into chatting away with her friends. But she stared out from the bus window that morning, looking directly at me.

I thought it was the beginning of the end. Now I see it was instead the beginning of the beginning.

Early on, we retreated to our corners. We ran on adrenaline. Initially it was the novelty of fear and disruption. When I was in high school I thought the world was boring. Our country in particular was especially boring, thanks a lot. Nothing exciting happened anymore. No Watergate, no big wars, no Woodstock, no *drama*.

But now:

Suddenly professional sports and Tom Hanks were down. Suddenly it was *batten down the hatches*. Let's attempt to comprehend an actual existential threat. Let's do what we said we always wanted to do—withdraw from everything and cancel every plan. And if you were awash in privilege, still had a (nonessential) job or a safety net, it also suddenly became this: *Let's learn something.* Let's give this meaning. Let's work on ourselves. This pandemic is an *opportunity.* Let's come out of this better than we were before.

It did not start well. We thought there were still rules, so we tried to stick to them and then snapped at each other when we failed. Sugar. Screens. Bedtimes. Wake-up times. Putting things away. Helping with the dishes. Homework. Chores. Interacting reasonably at all. On the same day I wrote an article for *The Cut* about how to work from home with kids, I yelled at my actual kids as they argued with each other, "LIKE I'M IN THE MOOD FOR THIS SHIT." Later that same day I announced to my family, but mostly to myself, "Don't judge how other people cope." Watch your shows, keep your bees, plant those seeds, get those abs of steel, bake that bread, honey.

Throughout the day, every day—what else was I going to do—I watched everyone's wheels come off on Instagram. Cloaked as insights or inspiration, truth-telling or transformation, every caption all but said, "Holy fuck you guys, we are fucked. I am fucked, you are fucked, humanity is fucked. Also? Turns out I want to choke the person I'm married to, I wish I could leave my kids behind forever, I hate my job, I am losing my fucking mind, what the fuck is happening." Our lives had been distracting us from our lives all along. The drinks and dinners, vacations and shopping, kids' sports and school plays, all that *leaving our houses*, had served to anesthetize us.

I was sucked into the darkest dens of pandemic humor on Twitter. I was assaulted on Facebook by senior photos from the 1980s as if any current high school senior gave a damn what anyone else's ancient experience was. I deactivated Facebook,

again. I was supposed to be writing a book, this book. Instead I
wrote bingo cards for *McSweeney's* and watched as two of them
went viral and that piece for *The Cut* went viral and I thought,
we really need a new word for that.

All the while, we were changing the subject. We all knew
what we feared most was death. We all knew we wanted to talk
about it but . . . not really. We all worried (we still worry) it would
come without being able to hold a hand, touch the hair, say, "I
love you. I forgive you. I will be okay, we will be okay." We all
feared we would have to say it or hear it through a screen, a dys-
topian nightmare.

What none of us wanted to admit was, if we avoided death
this time, what if this whole thing didn't mean anything? What
if we came out of this the same flawed, fucked-up people who
went in? What if everything didn't happen for a reason? What if
we weren't better? What if we're worse? What if we remain trau-
matized by a handshake, the thought of sweaty people jammed
into a club shoulder-to-shoulder, the entire concept of sticking
your tongue in someone's mouth who you haven't quarantined
with? What if we lose the shirts off our backs? What if we lose
our last scrap of hope?

I found myself, separately and spontaneously, wrapped up
in surprisingly casual conversations with my kids about death,
about what the point of life was. They were the ones who brought
this up, on their own. We lingered well past my bedtime, my self-
cut hair looking like it was styled by a typhoon. And I told them
in that way that parents do that, *ah yes*, this is a Big Question. A
lifelong question. I told them they were only at the beginning of
asking questions like this and they may never be satisfied with
the answers. And I told them that, as I got older, the only thing
I had finally figured out about life was it was only the day right

in front of me. It was all that was promised and even then, it was only promised minute-by-minute, like putting one foot in front of the other. When Jon and I were dating and I'd be spinning out about the unknowable future he'd respond, "One day at a time." It was a mantra his mother had adopted as she persevered through ovarian cancer. But I wanted actual answers. And his actual answer grated on me to the point that if I saw it coming I'd cut him off with a "I swear to god, don't 'one day at a time' me right now."

Now decades, a separation-without-end, and a global pandemic later, I had finally come around. Just look at our expectations! Look at all these plans we had made. Look at all these ghosts we had on our calendars. Look at the shadow lives we would've been leading if not for this. Look at everything we would've been complaining about that now we're desperate for, desperate for what it represents. Boring and predictable has never sounded so good. It's a hell of a thing to feel wistful about a dodged pelvic exam or a mundane text about who would pick the kids up from the school dance. What was the future anyway other than specific wishes, pinned on a grid that owed us nothing?

As April inexplicably arrived, somehow either five minutes or five years later, I found myself randomly feeling furious with my family and my circumstances. One time I walked out of my house and said only, "I'm leaving." I had to drive to get away. The walks I used to take to clear my head often left me angrier and more stressed. As spring finally threatened to arrive, bike paths became too crowded. I eyed every runner who puffed his way past me, every little kid on a bike who swerved within a foot of me, every dog still off its leash as the owner shouted, "He's friendly!," wondering if they were all coated in a fresh new plague.

My car became a one-woman spaceship that I launched into

the countryside. I got in and floored it in one direction until I was calm. I thought of all the places I wished I could stop along the way, the destination used to be the point. But now I just drove somewhere and back, keeping my contagion contained. One Saturday I drove to Vergennes, a ninety-minute round trip, blasting Radiohead until I gave myself a headache. Another Saturday, with the power of fury behind me, I made it almost to Rutland, an hour and a half away, before I calmed down.

My dog was with me so I stopped to let her out at a cemetery before we turned around and headed home. Cemeteries had become the only places I could collect my thoughts, the only places powerful enough to snap me out of my pity party bullshit. The sun was shining and this cemetery was empty, save the bones and souls I could not see. Wind chimes on graves caused me to whip around, looking for loose dogs.

I came across the weathered grave of a two-day-old baby who lived and died in 1950. *That was a different time,* I thought. As if death was solvable now. As if the reason I was in a cemetery an hour and a half away from home wasn't evidence to the contrary. I came across newer, more modern tombstones. For a girl only seven, a teenager born the same year as me, several twenty-year-olds lost to different wars. What was the point of any of it? What if the dead can't hear wind chimes? Who are all these Instagram posts for, these Twitter jokes, these bees and loaves and quads? We were launching ourselves into space, any way we could. We were sending transmissions to anyone who would listen. Can you hear me? Do you see me? Do I matter? Am I good? Will you remember me when I'm gone?

We made our way back toward my car where I had pulled off the narrow potholed road and onto grass stubborn enough to still believe in spring. A looming statue of Jesus with outstretched arms looked down on us. My dog growled and ran away from it, barking. She thought he was coming for us.

Jon turned fifty in April. The big blowout party we had planned to throw inside our house with a live band turned into two Zoom parties, one East Coast and one West, back when Zoom still felt novel and fun. No band. The West Coast version had been a surprise for him and it became clear within minutes all these faces that had been at our wedding and hadn't seen us together in person in at least ten years couldn't comprehend what in the actual hell we were doing. We were getting a divorce, they knew that, but we were sitting side by side chatting with them and laughing together, all of us shocked at the familiarity. Us looking at them, them looking at us, it had been so long. It was so wonderful and so weird. Was this a silver lining? It was the first time I thought, *wait, do pandemics even have those?*

Jon eventually lost his job, temporarily, when his employer shut down. Through a stroke of good fortune so (don't say unprecedented, don't say unprecedented) unprecedented (*damn it*), I had already landed the steadiest and most lucrative gig in my twelve years of freelancing. It was that arbitrary. It was that lucky.

I felt, and still feel, a shadow dread like the kind you experience when you come upon a fresh car crash. It's that feeling you get when you know it could've been you, had just one small thing gone differently. But it wasn't me, it wasn't us. Not this time. We could've gone under. My industry was collapsing as most industries were. A lifetime of cavalier financial decisions and my naïve belief that life would just keep feeding me money and achievement had left us in a precarious position. Only a year before I was waking up in the middle of the night, staring at the ceiling, wondering if we would have to sell our house. Not because of the divorce (although it would've made the perfect cover story), but because it would get us out from under the suffocating debt we had accumulated that was being compounded by my erratic and dwindling income. Yet unbelievably, here we were. As everything came apart in the world around us, everything came together for us. We once again had a common enemy.

With Jon out of work and a desire to keep busy, he looked the house over for projects. He did not need to look far. Over the previous three years I had come to think of the exterior of our house as a reflection of the interior of our relationship. It was in a state of disrepair and neglect, untended to and uninvested in. Early on we had yanked shrubs out from in front of our house with no plan and no money to replace them. We seeded wild-flowers and planted cheap annuals in their place and none of it looked intentional. I started referring to the style of our house as "haunted" because it was a funny way to cloak my embarrassment. But over the course of four months, with all his free time and all that money coming in, we set about remaking our house. And in the process we remade our relationship, too.

He fixed and repainted the ceiling of our front porch, installed a toilet and two air conditioners, cleaned and organized the basement and the garage. He built a raised bed in the front yard and planted two vegetable gardens bordered with flowers. He fastened two sets of new house numbers to the front and side of our house, numbers I had purchased the summer before. They had sat in their packages, dusty and ignored, on a side counter. He painted over their metal fronts with white paint so they'd pop, then he finished about fourteen other projects on top of that. With the first heat wave quickly approaching, we tracked down a 15-foot inflatable pool and he drove an hour round trip to grab the last one. He said, "You know what this thing needs? Inflatable chairs" and we bought those, too.

Even with all this—and this was plenty—he decided to paint the entire exterior of our house. This offer can't possibly mean anything to you if you've never owned a house. This offer can't possibly mean anything to you if you have siding that is maintenance-free. And this offer can't possibly mean anything to you unless you've ever gotten an estimate for having your house painted and thought, *wow, you have got to be fucking kidding me with this.*

I don't know how painting our house became the grandest gesture of all, but it was.

I picked colors and he painted swatches. He scraped flaking paint and filled holes where woodpeckers had done their worst and he spot-primed. Then he painted the entire exterior of the house, all 1,700 square feet of it, two coats. The trim and second story were suddenly a smooth, gleaming white. The rest of the house went from a flat light gray that was flaking and peeling to a deep, satiny charcoal gray that came out darker than I had intended. When Insta-pals saw photos of the house (how else were they going to see it?) they'd ask, "Wait, what color is that? Is that black or blue?" and I'd quote Batman from *The LEGO Movie,* "Very, very dark gray."

I felt proud every time I walked out the front door with the dog and looked back over my shoulder at the house, and just as proud every time I approached it on the return. I felt proud when I saw our family together, no matter which configuration we were in: in the driveway playing basketball, floating in our little cheap-ass pool, picking tomatoes from the garden. It was nice to feel proud again. I hadn't realized how much pride I had lost over time.

The summer of 2020 was one of the driest and hottest summers we had ever experienced in Vermont. Between June and July we had eighteen days that were 90 degrees or above, which placed it in the top five years containing the most 90 degree highs, dating back to the late 1800s. This is to be expected when civilization is ready to wrap things the fuck up.

For the first time since those summer days twenty-two years earlier in Portland, we had a small silly pool to fall into at the end of the day. And although we had two kids now, teenagers, their afternoon ban on screen time lifted at five o'clock so they'd rarely join us. We had originally bought this pool for all four of us, to have a safe place to cool off in case the beaches were a super-spreader nightmare. But usually it was just Jon and I bobbing around in there.

We started to refer to it as Adult Swim.

We would drift on our wonky floats and couldn't pat ourselves on the back enough for all of it—the pool, the inflatable chairs, the paint job, the money. We would drink cans of Free Flow IPA stuffed into koozies and stare up into the towering pines that shaded our pool. We didn't even need to apply sunscreen. We talked about work and our circle of friends, our kids and anything we wanted to really, because even though our neighbors could definitely see us and probably hear us, it somehow felt private. More than anything, we felt safe and grateful to be here. In Vermont, in our town, in our school district, in this house, and in our lives right at that moment.

Every single day I thought, *thank God this lockdown hadn't come two or three years earlier.* When we would've still been pretending to be happy, when we would've been sleeping in the same bed, when the sound of his chewing made me want to put my fist through a wall. And although I felt more trapped than I had before (understandable), I was surprised to discover I also felt relieved. I hadn't realized how much pressure I had felt to move on. Because that's what people did when they announced their divorce, right? They moved on? For the first time in a long time I was reminded of the pressure I had felt right after we got married, the pressure to get pregnant. But within that first year of our marriage we eventually stepped back and decided, you know what, we definitely do *not* need to do this right now. So we didn't.

The pressure to move on was gone because where were any of us going? This big house with too much room that had been the albatross around our necks almost from the minute we bought it suddenly seemed like the best decision we had ever made. Six years after we moved in and while we were mid-separation, I finally settled in.

In the first year after we announced our divorce, I was angry but tried so hard to seem like I wasn't. I blamed Jon while trying to act like I wasn't doing that at all. I put on a big performance of what I thought I had done wrong but, deep down, I was still furious. I felt like nobody in my life had ever fought to keep me. That when I said I was leaving, everyone, every single time, all but said, *fine, go.* I felt like nobody ever stood up for me and I was so sick of standing up for myself.

It's hard to parse the emotions that happen at the end of anything—getting fired, someone dying, a friendship combusting, a marriage dissolving. It's easy to forget anything good came before. It's easy to think the signs of your future destruction were so obvious. It's easy to blame or self-flagellate when, really, this is just what life is. It is a series of ups and downs and near misses that are unpredictable. We make choices that are contrary to our beliefs or long-term interests. We want more and settle for less. We want less and sign up for more. We bump around and hold

fast to our expectations as if they are contracts. We think out-
comes are guaranteed as long as we have witnesses. We want
people to change but only in the specific ways we approve of.
We make different sets of rules, one for us, one for our partners.
That's what Jon actually used to call it when we were dating
and first married: "Oh, different rules. I see." For example, it was
okay if he drank as long as I was drinking but if I was trying to
cut back suddenly *his* drinking was the problem. We focus on
fairness, insofar as it's fair to us individually.

We are afraid of what other people think, even when we
say we aren't. We want people to love us and hold us, cherish
and fight for us, even when we sometimes don't feel like doing the same for them. We want to be special even when we
think other people are ordinary. We want to be right because
that would mean everyone else is wrong. We want everything to
work out, even when we don't understand what "working out"
even means.

I was raised without boundaries and then I blamed the person I married for imposing none. I quit every job where someone
exerted too much control over me and then I got mad at the
person I married because he rarely took control away from me. I
lived my life doing whatever I wanted and then I married someone who let me do whatever I wanted and I was furious with him
toward the end of our marriage because of it. I married a person
who told me verbatim, in a letter the same week as our wedding,
that he didn't know how to communicate or express his feelings
and then I spent the end of our marriage enraged that he didn't
know how to communicate or express his feelings. I married
a person who seemed nothing like my parents, nothing at all,
but everything he unwittingly did felt familiar, it felt like home.
What he did was what I knew. And since he was right here next

to me, how convenient it became to blame him for absolutely everything.

I used to think the story of our demise was that of a victim and a villain. That he was the good guy and I was the bad. But nothing is ever that simple. What if I stayed in my marriage because I was afraid to feel like a failure? What if I hadn't done anything better than my parents had after all—and everyone found out? What if I was only getting more ambitious over time and I knew the only way I'd retain the flexibility and freedom I needed to pursue my own goals was within the structure of this particular marriage? What if I had married this man because I loved him and I knew in my gut he would be a good father? Is that a crime? What if I pushed him to be more ambitious, too, and gave him a life that was perhaps better than it would've been otherwise? What if I wasn't a perfect mother but certainly a good one? What if I could just stop making everything such a big fucking deal?

None of this shit will matter one day, I tried to remind myself.

None of this shit will matter when I'm in a box in the ground, a dried-out wreath still on my grave from Christmas, or a fistful of ash in the ocean. None of this will matter when wind chimes chime to a stranger and her dog as they walk toward a looming statue of Jesus with his Jonathan Van Ness hair. None of this will matter when that dog walks straight through my ghost and feels stranger danger for Jesus, the only thing that made perfect sense anymore.

It has now been two years since Jon and I announced our divorce. We don't owe each other anything marriage-wise but we do owe each other humanity-wise. What we have done has worked, mostly. We know it won't work forever. We continued on with our marriage under a much less certain outcome than this. This experience has been both boring and a spin cycle of emotion. But it could've been worse. Everyone expected it to be worse. *Are people disappointed this isn't worse?* is a question I ponder often.

We're still navigating an uncharted, and sometimes emotional, obstacle course. In the year before the pandemic, I attended my cousin's bridal shower on a perfect spring day and didn't completely lose my shit, wanting to warn everyone to get their heads out of their asses already. The night before her wedding that September, all of us packed into a bar for whiskey and pool, I yelled to her friend who'd be performing the ceremony, "I think marriage is stupid but I am *PUMPED* for this wedding!" And when I saw random brides and grooms out in public I successfully refrained from screaming *DON'T DO IT*. This is the social contract.

You can't just hover around the edges of every marriage-adjacent event like some sort of weird Divorce Witch. People will keep climbing this ladder of adulthood no matter what you do or say. Even if you're standing right next to it holding a sign over your head that reads THIS LADDER IS FUNDAMENTALLY BROKEN AND ALSO: IT SUCKS. People will keep falling in love, they will keep getting married, and they will keep having kids. And you can tell people all you want about everything that could go wrong but no one will listen. *You* wouldn't have listened. What did it have to do with *you*? You would've thought anyone who tried to warn you was just bitter. They didn't understand how unique and exquisite your love was; how next-level your future children would be.

We celebrated our anniversary, our 22nd, together. I thought about how we had avoided September 17th as our wedding date because it was my parents' wedding date and I didn't want that for our kids, or for us. We had nothing to be ashamed of. I didn't want to avoid talking about our wedding, our anniversary, or our marriage. Just because we didn't want our kids to pattern their own romantic relationships after our marriage didn't mean there wasn't something of value there. It didn't have to mean, well, there goes the bathwater. Better hand me that baby, I guess.

Jon made his mom's manicotti recipe, as he did every year. He poured wine for the two of us. And we all sat around our big dining room table, the table where we had fed our babies tiny spoonfuls of pureed turkey and applesauce. The table where they had blown out candles on their birthday cakes year after year after year. The table where people we loved and who loved us would gather at holidays. And we told our kids about what an amazing day October 4th, 1997, had been. It was one of the best days of my life, one of the best days of his. We didn't have any doubts, I truly did not, I said, even though the sky was cloudy and I couldn't get out of my head long enough to hear my dad telling me I looked beautiful. Couldn't he feel the rain?

It was a date that still deserved to be celebrated. Because it was more than just the date of a wedding, a big party, for two hopeful fools in their twenties who didn't know any better. It was the beginning of our family, too. Long before we knew we would have these two kids, we began our lives together, full of excitement and hope. So we toasted to October 4th, two glasses of wine, one glass of water, one glass of milk. I still can't believe I didn't cry. It was a moment of hope in a year that inexplicably contained many.

When I had finally moved upstairs to my own room— only four months before the lockdown and almost a year after announcing our divorce—I watched as Jon assembled my bed frame and had our son help. These moments of grace accumulated like snow in a squall. I snuck a photo of them joining the frame together, doing the work necessary to help move me away from them, even if for now it was just one floor away. Sadness still coursed through this transition, of course. It was the first tangible reminder that, yes, this was still the path we were on.

I have spent almost the entirety of our separation writing and thinking about marriage and divorce. I have read books I likely wouldn't have read otherwise. I delved into my past in a way I can't imagine doing were it not for this book. I came to the announcement of our separation angry and fed up even though I tried to seem super cool about it. I was mad at him and mad at myself. I felt stupid for not seeing this coming way back when we first met. How could I not see into the future?

It's human nature to focus on what is right in front of our faces most of the time, believing no other perspective is possible. We let our disappointment or sadness or anger trigger our personal mythology repeatedly. Whatever we've believed about ourselves, especially the bad stuff, we double down on. Of course this is happening. Of course it is! What did I expect? Stupid bitch. But in taking the long view I've found myself coming to surprising and, fine I'll just say it, comforting conclusions.

From the time I was a teenager I had been begging the universe to love me. Please love me. But more than that, care for me. Make me feel cared for. Send me a handsome boy I can love and care for, too. Send me someone who will bring me flowers and remember my birthday and all the other crap teenage girls wished for based on popular culture in the mid-1980s. I didn't know screenwriters wrote those stories based on a predictable narrative arc and audiences demanded happy endings. I didn't know magazines written for girls and women were driven by advertising dollars and the content contained within them was mostly the same shit over and over again, just repackaged for different seasons. I didn't know most of my ideas about love and what it meant to be a woman were being shaped by people who had things to sell me and money to make.

Regardless, I had asked the universe for someone to love me. And I was loved. I begged to belong, to be accepted, to have a good life. I have belonged, I have been accepted, I have had a good life. And although within a week of announcing our divorce, a friend from our Portland days relayed to me that Jon and I "had always been an awkward match" (!!!) we made it damn far with that awkward match, thank you very much. We built a life far beyond what we imagined when we were first engaged, living in a small apartment with hand-me-down furniture and a kitchen the size of a walk-in closet.

This man has been a miracle in my life, that's what I've concluded. What I believe now, in looking so far back and through everything I wrote when I was a teenager and in my twenties, is I had multiple opposing desires: I wanted to live independently and have sex whenever I felt like it but I also wanted someone to prove to me they loved me enough to marry me. And I always wanted children, even though plenty of men have felt completely comfortable telling me I didn't seem like "the maternal type."

Could my marriage literally have been defined as passive aggressive (him passive, me aggressive)? The answer is yes. It was a perfect combination until it wasn't. It was a perfect combination until I wanted him to be someone he would never be, couldn't be, and had no interest in being. And he never asked me to be anyone other than who I was.

He has never said an unkind word to me. He has never said a negative word about my body. I don't think he's ever even called me a bitch and if you know me, that's something right there. It should go without saying, but I'll say it, he has never raised a hand to me, never shoved me even gently. This isn't where the bar should be set. It just shouldn't. These shouldn't be good boy points. But I've known plenty of men who consider themselves to be good men and have done at least one of those things with a partner at some point. I can't think of a single woman I know who has never seen a man (a father, a partner, a brother) punch a wall.

When I talk about Jon and all his positive qualities—of which there are obviously many—someone will always ask, "Why don't you stay with him then?" Let's back up to where the weight of this question rests. When people ask me why we don't just stay together if everything is so damn wonderful, the weight is always on me. But the marriage itself, the weight of so much of it, had already been on me since the beginning. I was tired of carrying that weight. So often women are made to feel responsible for the work needing to be done in a marriage. Being passive, akin to civil disobedience, in a marriage does not automatically make you the better partner. It puts the weight of every decision and your joint trajectory all onto one person. Not participating in the nurturing and reflection around a relationship is not the same as being a success at that relationship. Only in marriage would nonparticipation, non-rocking-the-boat count as doing a bang-up job.

So it isn't fair to me to give him all the credit. My ambition and my work have allowed him to have a life I don't think he would've had otherwise. I pushed him to be more ambitious, to think about what he wanted to do as his life's work. I questioned him being a-okay with a good enough job with virtually no opportunity to learn or advance. I pushed him to think big, that I would carry us financially, that I wanted him to feel fulfilled and happy. I had forgotten I had told him, back when we were dating, that I wanted to write, earn most of the money, maybe even earn enough that he could be the one to stay home with our future children. He felt swept away by that. Not insulted, not outraged, but swept away. It sure feels like a big detail to forget.

Without me, our family doesn't exist. Of course it took both of us to conceive our children. But at the end of the day my body endured years of birth control, four pregnancies, two miscarriages, an attempted external cephalic version, two C-sections, cracked nipples, two years of breastfeeding two children who had two completely different sets of nursing challenges—latching and nipple shields and blood coming from where blood just should never come from—and the looming consequences of an almost complete absence of birth control since I refused to get an IUD inserted after a painful attempt and he refused to get a vasectomy. When I reread that list, it frankly makes me want to dynamite the entire Earth, even still.

I have been on the hook as the emotional midwife for three people and an entire marriage. I have relished it in many ways. It *has* been healing. But it has also been exhausting. So where does this leave me? Where does it leave us? I can feel clear-eyed and still grateful. I can appreciate what has worked and can (mostly) let go of what hasn't. I can hold multiple truths in my head and heart simultaneously. When it comes to the dissolution of other people's marriages, more people should give this concept a whirl.

One thing I've discovered throughout this process is people who stay married and are struggling want to know there is suffering in divorce. They aren't conscious of this wanting, but it's there all the same. They want to know the alternative is so much worse than what they're currently dealing with. They like to imagine there is some sort of reward at the end of their stress and strife, a cookie for toughing it out. That, simply put, the moral high ground will always be theirs.

So when they see we are not suffering, and I will speak for myself here, nowhere near as much as I was suffering when I was married and pretending to be happy, performing what a good marriage looks like, they aren't sure what to make of it. The narrative arc around divorce only tilts toward the extremes, so imagine my surprise that, for once in my life, I am backstroking through the gray areas. These stories don't get told because, guess what, they're boring. Where's the tension?

Oh don't worry, there's still plenty.

I used to believe life was a straight line containing a series of stages. And within each stage there was a beginning, middle, and end. But what I've discovered is life is instead a series of loops, growing in circumference and range as we age, always finding a way to deposit us right back on land we thought we had long ago left behind.

At first I dreaded reading my high school and college diaries because the story I had told myself as time went on was I was just a dumb girl who liked dumb bands, dumb boys, and had dumb dreams. I told myself I would run away, to be smarter and cooler, to be more pure and have better ideas. I would be honest, always, even though women were never rewarded for honesty. I would be a better mother and a better partner and I would never have limits on my love. My parents and my friends and every man I had ever been with had limits and I had never forgiven any of them for it.

As much as I initially cringed through the level of detail in some of my entries, tempted to wing each and every one of those notebooks into Lake Champlain (look, I jotted down that I had held a man's gold necklace in my teeth while he fucked me, a man I recall not at all, and there's nothing I can do about that now), there was one takeaway from all of it.

I was always in there.

I had always been me.

As I committed to plow through one diary after another instead of dip in and out of them weeks or months apart, a more accurate portrait than the one I remembered began to take shape. I stopped cringing and started appreciating. I wasn't as dumb as I thought I had been nor was I as unhappy. Even though I felt neglected or alone in some ways, I sought out other supports and relationships that enriched my life and kept me safe. I wasn't as exclusively focused on being in a relationship as I had remembered. I wrote about sex a lot and clearly in some unsparing detail (oof, but also, some of it was kind of hot?). I was just trying to understand the world and my place within it. I was just trying to be happy and I was happy, often. Sometimes as I read I would lightly touch a page, feeling the indentations of ballpoint pen made thirty-four years ago and think, *I see you* and then *you know what, you really are okay, you really will be okay.*

When Jon and I met and fell in love, I stopped writing in a journal. I only wrote sporadically in those first two or three years and then I didn't write in a journal again. The story I had told myself for years was that I stopped writing because I was finally happy. The perception I had of my diaries back then was that I was lost and sad because I was alone. I was a single girl just crying into my notebooks, pathetic really. But rereading them showed me that wasn't true at all. I was just trying to figure out who I was, what I wanted, and just as importantly, what I didn't want. I now wish I had kept writing. I wish I had kept trying to figure out who I was when Jon and I were dating, throughout our marriage, when our children were born and when they were little, and even when things started to come apart. I wish I had never handed the job over to someone else, no matter how much I had loved him. It should've never been his job in the first place.

Two months into lockdown a listing had gone up through our neighborhood Front Porch Forum, which is like Nextdoor for Vermont. It offered a cottage on the lake, now being rented only to Vermonters during the pandemic. I clicked on the link and saw a 1930s cottage with a view of the water that reminded me of the Maine cottages where I would stay as a teenager and in college, and more recently the one we returned to every summer with our kids. I responded immediately and within two days I had booked a week for us in August, a month I wasn't totally sure would exist.

When we arrived at that cottage, on a hot Saturday afternoon, the first week in an August that existed, we did what we always did. We ran to the biggest window to gawk at the view and then quickly set about putting away just enough of our stuff so we could crack a beer, change into swimsuits, and get into that water. I made the beds and Jon put the groceries away. I set aside the sheets and a pillow and blanket for him on the foldout couch since he was only staying for a couple nights. I splayed across the queen bed with a view of the lake. We were out of the house. *We were finally out of our goddamn beautiful house.*

Jon and the kids set off on kayaks and in a canoe for the floating dock in the middle of the lake. I drank a beer and read a book and had not another thing on my mind. After a year of freelancing full time and trying to write this book simultaneously, it was finally the beginning of my abbreviated summer, when all I had to do was sleep, write, eat, read, and write more. I felt like my brain, my gut, and my heart were finally able to unclench. I felt like I was finally in a place that wasn't completely circumscribed by a screen and a keyboard. It felt like a normal summer day in The Before, somehow even better perhaps because I appreciated it more, and I thought I would pop.

We gobbled pasta caprese made with tomatoes from our garden for dinner and watched the sky turn indigo. We built a fire and I had my first s'more of the season even though it was, as previously stated, somehow August already. I had missed strawberry season and would soon miss blueberry season and probably all the white corn, too. I began to wonder if I shouldn't just let go of the things I did every summer, especially the things I used to do with our kids. Maybe it was time to stop holding on so damn tight to rituals and tradition. Nothing was going to be the same again, not for anyone, not after this year.

Jon and I sat by the fire later that night, in pools of silence. The kids had gone to bed an hour or two before and the lake was dark and quiet save for a yellow glow from three cottages dotted around the lake and a boat returning from dinner or drinks elsewhere.

I had wanted to ask Jon a question since early in the pandemic, when I couldn't imagine even hugging someone new never mind putting my tongue—or anything else—in another person's mouth. It had been years since I felt nervous asking him anything, so my mouth would fall open, then close, like a guppy in the darkness. We finally had come to a place of balance, where we knew our places. This was working.

And I risked all of that.

"Can I ask you a question and I promise not to get mad if you say 'no'?"

"Oh boy. Uh, okay?" was Jon's response.

"Would you ever have sex with me? For, you know, practical reasons?"

It was my first conversation about consent.

I woke up the next morning and stretched out in my bed alone, lifted my head to peer out at the lake. I went to use the bathroom and there was blood on the toilet paper when I pulled it away, likely the remnants of a recent period. I preferred to believe that after two years I had basically lost my virginity again.

I quietly made a cup of coffee while the three of them slept, attempting to make sense of an unfamiliar coffee maker without my glasses on. I slipped through the screen door, careful to hold it as it tried to snap shut, and I walked down to the dock. I stretched out and felt fuzzy, a feeling I hadn't felt in so long. My fingertips still buzzed, my head in the clouds. A mildly pleasant hangover deadened my nerves and all my thoughts. Sun warmed my body as caffeine began to course through it. I was covered in bug bites and my knees were scraped from the night before. I had stared up at the star-filled sky and the passing charcoal clouds at midnight as the cottages on either side of us sat silent and dark. The two of us, alone, on a blanket in the grass. Had we ever even had sex outside before? Did camping count? I guess it did.

I hadn't been thinking about love or marriage or what my body looked like or how old it was in those moments. I only thought about how every single touch felt electric and desired, and how this part at least did not need to be complicated. I could stand to think less, maybe. Could I just feel good? Could I just have this? I felt the desperation and fear drain out of me. I didn't fall back in love. I wasn't trying to and I didn't. That doesn't mean it meant nothing.

Sworn to secrecy, I told exactly one friend what had happened. It reminded her of something her aunt had once told her. This aunt had been divorced in her twenties, involved with a series of terrible men after, and then spent many years alone. When she found a partner she adored in her mid-fifties, she said to my friend, her adult niece who by then was married, "I'm tired of pretending sex isn't important."

So was I.

I was finally on my way back to me.

The honeymoon of my divorce is over. We are no closer to being divorced than we were when I started this book, but it is still the path we are on. We love one another but are not *in* love with one another. We are friends, so there are boundaries. Our expectations are more reasonable, our efforts more appreciated. We still disagree, but everything doesn't feel at stake when we do. We are more willing to try new things or do small things differently because we're already doing the biggest thing differently that we can imagine. We've created a kinship that isn't problem-free nor can it replace the intimacy of a deep romantic partnership. But it is so much better than what I expected and feared, all those years ago, when I felt our marriage slipping away.

So, to answer my own questions when I started writing this book: No, we are not living in separate houses nor are we in separate states. Yes, we are living upstairs and downstairs from each other, sometimes sitting together at meals. And no, we didn't take our vacation together in Maine.

We tried.

We had paid—in full and a year in advance—to rent a new

place at our usual beach the third week of August. We watched the COVID stats and the colors of counties on travel maps as the summer wore on. A week before our trip, green meant GO. We had our mail held, put our dog in a kennel, watered all the plants before we left. When we arrived after five hours of driving, to the best oceanfront view of that beach I had ever had in my life, driving down a private dirt road I hadn't even allowed myself to walk down before and past the beautiful old homes I had envied since I was nine, we discovered that the oceanfront cottage we had rented was somehow also a *shared* cottage and somehow that detail had not been . . . shared.

Only two and a half weeks earlier a woman had been killed by a great white shark off an island just seven miles from that beach. The details had all been there in the news, her being jerked down in the water and tossed in the air, right in front of her daughter who had fallen to her knees, screaming. I couldn't begin to fathom it. It was the first fatal shark attack in Maine state history, all that childhood tomfoolery back in Rhode Island came rushing back to me. Still, I had held on through all of it, willing my way through. *This is just what we did every summer.* And now I was standing on a shared deck with a man who took his mask off and shook my son's hand before revealing he had already had COVID. When they expressed their confusion that we didn't know that we'd all be staying there at the same time (granted, on separate floors), using the same common outdoor spaces and we should trust them, *we wouldn't even know they were there*, I shout-muffled through my mask, "WHAT ARE YOU TALKING ABOUT? WE'RE IN THE MIDDLE OF A GLOBAL PANDEMIC." *We know you're here.*

Of course, it was a beautiful day, a perfect day really. Jon leaned over and said, "How about we walk over to the car" and I could feel every moment of our horrible, wonderful year. Every moment of beauty and melancholy. Every moment of fear and grace. I got into my car, turned the steering wheel hard left and gunned it, spitting sand and rocks behind me. I thought of all the diaries I had filled up writing about this beach, how it returned me to myself over and over again. And now it was just one more thing to let go of, at least for now. God, fuck this place.

We arrived back at our house twelve hours after we had left. We had taken both our cars because we do not travel light on this vacation. Jon threw all the firewood he had brought for beach fires across our lawn so he could get to the cooler and yelled, "Want fifteen beers? Because they're ice cold." We unpacked both vehicles because that's just what we did after trips, even twelve-hour ones. And then someone, probably my daughter, said, "I think we need a group hug" and we hugged in our dining room. I announced, "Kids, I hope you will remember this forever, the absolute dumbest day of our lives as a family." We sat on the couch and sort of stared at each other, still stunned, but at least we started to find parts of the story funny even though only hours earlier they had seen me driving away from that beach, silent, with tears plinking down on my dress.

The next day we checked the travel map. The county we had been in had turned yellow while we were there. We had to quarantine for fourteen days, for a vacation we didn't even take.

After all this, this is where I leave you:

I don't know how or, more accurately, when this arrangement will finally end.

But I do know I asked the universe to be loved, to be happy.

I have been loved. I have been happy.

I am loved. I am happy.

I have read and thought and talked and reminisced and cried, although less of that last one than I expected. I sifted through boxes of wedding and honeymoon mementos, rediscovered twenty-five years of photos and anniversary cards. I found my wedding planner and our honeymoon travel dispatches and portraits of us as a new family. I snacked on Peppermint Patties, those silvery wrappers still somehow a promise, as I watched videos of our little kids running in circles in our kitchen, my daughter following after my son like a little chicken. I saw in those moments we didn't fail more than anyone else, and we didn't do better than anyone else. We did the best we could with what we knew. We tried to have a good life together and we did. We loved each other for a long time.

How can I be anything but grateful?

So this is it. The end of another book. A closed chapter in my life. I've written all I've experienced and gone through. A jumbled confusion of emotions. Pride, jealousy, love, hate, hurt, all there. Maybe not for the world to see, but it felt like it. So now I leave this book behind. And maybe someday someone will read it all and try to understand me. And then they'll realize the task doesn't get any easier no matter how much inside information you have.

—*August 22, 1985, 16 years old*

Reading List

I read these books during the process of writing the book you now hold in your hands. Some were brand-new blockbusters and others were older obscure titles I found in used bookstores or on dollar shelves and I liked their covers (sometimes it pays to judge books by them). These books expanded my worldview; provided desperately needed personal perspective, historical perspective, or life guidance; confirmed a few things I suspected; exploded long-held assumptions and showed me where those long-held assumptions had originally taken root; or took me on quite the range of wild rides.

Reading *Generation* X, twenty-nine years and about three lifetimes after I read it the first time, singlehandedly made the case for rereading books I thought were perhaps too dated or stereotypically "of my generation." I found myself thinking often as I read certain scathing lines, *whew we didn't know the half of it.*

I urge you to seek out each and every one of these books and, if I may be so bold, to write one of your own. Even if it's just for you. Especially then.

Fleishman Is in Trouble by Taffy Brodesser-Akner
Does Monogamy Work? by Luke Brunning
Making Marriage Work: A History of Marriage and Divorce in the
    Twentieth-Century United States by Kristin Celello

When Things Fall Apart: Heart Advice for Difficult Times by Pema Chödrön

Marriage, A History: How Love Conquered Marriage by Stephanie Coontz

The Way We Never Were: American Families and the Nostalgia Trap by Stephanie Coontz

Generation X: Tales for an Accelerated Culture by Douglas Coupland

The Problem That Has No Name by Betty Friedan

Maybe You Should Talk to Someone: A Therapist, Her Therapist, and Our Lives Revealed by Lori Gottlieb

All the Rage: Mothers, Fathers, and The Myth of Equal Partnership by Darcy Lockman

Self-Help by Lorrie Moore

The Second Journey: Spiritual Awareness and the Mid-Life Crisis by Gerald O'Collins

Mating in Captivity: Unlocking Erotic Intelligence by Esther Perel

The State of Affairs: Rethinking Infidelity by Esther Perel

American Women: Our Spirituality in Our Own Words by Catherine Racette and Peg Reynolds

Ordinary Love & Good Will by Jane Smiley

Flash Count Diary: Menopause and the Vindication of Natural Life by Darcey Steinke

Acknowledgments

First of all, I wrote a book about divorce during a global pandemic and the near fall of democracy, so *thanks to me*. But enough about me (theoretically).

Thank you to my agent Ryan Harbage, who's the king of fielding my half-assed pitches and giving me an unfiltered thumbs up or thumbs down. Thank you, again, for finding me in the wilds of the internet.

Profound gratitude to everyone at Harper Perennial for believing in me a second time. Thank you to Stephanie Hitchcock for initially bringing this book on board (and for being the last person I attended live theater with, *sob*) and to Doug Jones, Amy Baker, Lisa Erickson, Heather Drucker, Kristin Cipolla, Kim Daly, Hayley Salmon for promptly scratching every project management itch I've had, and Jen Heuer for the brilliant cover.

I have immense appreciation for my editor, Sarah Stein, who came to our arranged marriage with an open mind and sharp notes, even when she had to deliver the sharpest of those notes the same week Elizabeth Warren dropped out of the presidential race and the pandemic hit. It! Was! Not! A! Great! Week! For! Sharp! Notes! I'm in awe of your willingness to take this book on and work so hard to make it the best it could possibly be.

Big thanks to Riane Konc who brilliantly edited the humor

pieces—proving she's as much of an assassin as an editor as she is a writer—and also gifted me with the phrase "sex reasons."

Thank you to *Seven Days* for giving me an opportunity (and a deadline) to craft the foundation of what would become the epilogue. Thanks also to Matt Soniak and *Mental Floss* for allowing me to excerpt "The Horrors of Anglerfish Mating," which helped crystallize so much of my experience with . . . so much.

One of the delightful aspects of working on this book was having an excuse to fact-check utter nonsense from my past. Although many of those moments didn't make it into the final book, big thanks are due to Malinda Moller, Karla Hull, Ted Paduck, and especially Bob Richards, who did a lovely and funny interview about our whirlwind two-week "relationship" in high school. I'm sorry I was such a bitch to you in the cafeteria when we were in college.

It was a hot year for facts, so highly accurate thanks to Michelle Harris for fact-checking a humor piece, of all things. And for reminding me about emergency breakthroughs, which ended up in the final version of "What to Expect When You're Expecting to Be a GenX Girl."

I've desperately missed writing in places other than my house, so I'm waving and mouthing *thank you* to New Moon Café, Philo Ridge Farm, The Great Northern, and Maglianero here in Vermont; Lincolnville Motel and The Francis in Maine; and the TWA Hotel, Ace Hotel NYC, and random business traveler hotels all over Cupertino.

I'm incredibly grateful to have had a group of readers who pulled no punches and some of those fuckers punched hard. Thank you to Mary Adkins, Toby Barlow, Cris Dabica, Emily Flake, Riane Konc, and Rachel Livsey for your smart notes, direct challenges, and enthusiastic encouragement. Special thanks are owed to Darren Higgins, Amanda Levinson, and Jennifer Romolini who reviewed multiple drafts, surgically pinpointed weaknesses (and suggested solutions), and delivered all of that with loads of empathy. I'm forever grateful for the time and attention you each gave this book.

Amanda Levinson deserves an extra shout out for initiating an (almost) daily voice memo exchange two and a half years ago. Since then she's served as my unpaid therapist, book sounding board, talkin'-'bout-marriage conversational partner, one-person global pandemic/fall of democracy support group, and a great friend. Yapping aloud into my phone every day became a way of working out my thoughts and she was the source of crucial book-changing and life-changing insights. Amanda, thank you for absolutely everything.

I owe my longtime work partner and super friend, Michael Dabbs, a huge debt of gratitude. You've bridged this phase of my marriage effortlessly and never took sides, loving us both. You've always been more than a work partner (and someone I hit up for author website redesigns and bingo card layouts). You will always be family, even if it's kind of messed up that my kids call you Uncle Dads.

Words are insufficient to thank my own personal coven, Amanda Gustafson, Jen O'Neill, and Meg Rupert. I cannot begin to fathom what the past decade would've been like without the three of you. It's a rare group of women who can share fears, joys, and everyday sorrows and trust that the counsel will be wise, loving, and funny as shit. It doesn't hurt that you're all hot as hell and class up any joint you walk into. It's been so hard to not hug you for a year. I love you all, so much.

To Hawthorne and Walker, thank you for showing up for me, again and again and in the most surprising ways. Nothing

I've accomplished in my life comes close to how proud I am of the funny, tender, creative, and wise people you've always been and the startlingly tall full-fledged adults you're becoming. Don't forget to vote!

To Jon, what is there left to say (maybe it'd be great if I stopped saying things now?!) other than *thank you*. Thank you for trusting me throughout the high-wire act of creating this book. Thank you for always believing in me. Thank you for the life we've made—and continue to make—together. Thank you for our kinship.

To Edie, if any dog could read acknowledgements, it'd be you.